I0083191

The Guide

A 28-day Meditative Cycle

KEVIN HASZTO

Illustrated by Emily Haszto

The Guide: A 28-day Meditative Cycle

Copyright ©2022 Kevin Haszto
All rights reserved. First edition 2022

No part of this book may be reproduced or transmitted in any form
or by any means, electronic or mechanical, including photocopying,
recording or by any information storage and retrieval system,
without permission in writing from the publisher.

Produced in the United States of America

First Edition, paperback version
ISBN 978-1-7333237-1-0

1. Spirit writings. 2. Self-realization—Miscellanea.
3. Channeling (Spiritualism)

Published by SageSong Press LLC
email: sagesongpress@gmail.com

Printed by Lulu.com in the United States

Cover Design by Kevin Haszto.
Illustrations by Emily Haszto.

For my wife, Kumiko: a loving, patient, and helpful partner to me and a support system throughout the years for our entire family—Thank you for the encouragement on this project and for helping me to find the time to devote to it. I love you.

♡

Contents

Acknowledgments
Preface
Introduction

WEEK 1: Core Practice

DAY 1: Direct Observing Within   2
awareness | directing attention | objects of experience |
self as I | context, relationship, achievement, structure,
survival as a focus | concepts | God | I Am | observation
| receiving life | will | self-abidance | God within

DAY 2: Working Without   6
attributes of consciousness | filters | inner & outer |
meditation | stillness | duality | limiting your activity
| prayerful intent | inner work | outer work | obstacles &
movement | sensation & perceptions | vision | purpose |
choose again

DAY 3: Illusion and the Ego Dance   14
belief in ego needs | ego analysis | belief in illusions |
incremental healing | appreciation & forgiveness |
incremental activity | true gold | need not prepare |
understand with your intellect | release | admitting you
don't know

DAY 4: Invention   18
the world you see | creative vision | grasping or aversion
| joy | triune nature | concepts have a use | the ego's
framework | holiness & specialness | aspects

DAY 5: Strength and Vision   22
your true nature | highest forms | removing blocks |
higher self | evolutionary tree of Father, Son, Holy
Spirit | heaven | lower self | I always speak | call to
integrate the shadow | waiting patiently | ego is decider |
choose yet again

DAY 6:   Positive Intent in Action   28
          positive action | appropriate loving activity | infinite
          blessing | complete harmlessness | evidence of guilt |
          claim your own | teach Love

DAY 7:   Living Truth   32
          awakened to truth | lifeforce as truth | context of the
          higher self | every step of the journey | walking each
          other home | where you see yourself | first call | fingers
          pointing

WEEK 2:   Extension of Practice

DAY 8:   Chasing Effects and Substitutes   38
          awareness-of-awareness | nothing special | freewill |
          dampens ability to experience | tools | one true desire |
          excitement | everything drops away | perceiving outside
          of God | clear light | between dreams | the final step

DAY 9:   The Cord as Code   44
          always tethered | paradox | the trinity unified | world is
          animated | no effort | life in flow | the code | giving
          to God | lack of success | sinking down | in union |
          a canvas | by God or in God | the Sun | play

DAY 10:   Extending Presence   48
          mind & heart searching | image | helps it unfold |
          self-reflection | misidentified | zero-sum game | basis
          for grander ideas | personhood clothes it | way of
          seeing | One Light | roles | your agreements | shared
          unlimited being

DAY 11:   Pause for Feeling   52
          feel God's light | energy center | lifeforce | do not attach

DAY 12:   Alignment of Thought   54
          three modes | hide-and-seek | aligned with I Am | the
          innocent mind | pouring Love | new innocence

DAY 13:   Shared Consciousness   58
          an aspect of you | the power of your mind | what you
          think is real | a potential for insanity | the remembering |
          a mental state | clear & reset | fear not | shared thoughts |
          patch of blue sky | clouds come back

DAY 14:   The Implication for the Universe   62
          connected to One Source | neighbors | singular
          framework | you cannot leave the creation | each sun is
          an experiment | lifeforce manifesting | no value in
          defense | greater acceptance | as a soul evolves it
          focuses | groups of seven | social memory complex |
          forgotten song | astral plane | shared dream | teeming
          with life | the body is not the self | causal plane | degrees
          of freedom | experiment of expression

WEEK 3:   Transformation and Consistency of Practice

DAY 15:   Forgiveness   70
          God does not condemn | release yourself from illusions
          | the grudge | illusion about yourself | no apology is
          needed | you hold the key | demanding payment | laugh
          or cry | I forgive myself | condemnation | gratifying your
          ego | others as a means | only proper response | opening
          to you | laying down the debt | your decision | mistaking
          your brother | effects of your own poison | fracture of
          your world | Love will wait

DAY 16:   Self-Acceptance and Self-Care   76
          enjoy where you are | large offenses | hard to balance |
          entrusted to care for | bless the world | serious parts |
          reconnect | naturally constructive

DAY 17:   Seeing into Perception   80
          slow it down & allow space | experience lucidity | the
          form of visuals | captivate us or carry us away | listening
          & receiving | mind's eye | focus on my voice | have a
          conversation | find time

DAY 18:   The Blessed Distraction   84
startling sensations | channels of energy | physical activity | ecstatic experiences | diversion from the path | accessed directly | an ambassador | applying the attributes | less sober of mind | voluntary sensory deprivation | three types of thought expression | internal chatter | inner orgasm | tantric & yogic | rhythmic auditory driving | fantasy or daydream

DAY 19:   God with You   90
old releases resurface | many substitutes | clever covering | the why | loneliness & abandonment | unleashes your joy within | don't yet see it | attraction of bodies | love unconditionally | leave appearances | look outward to achieve

DAY 20:   Trust   94
trust in the possibility | take time to notice | depending on compatibility | choose differently | new opportunities | peace will arise | simplest recognition | the mountains didn't paint themselves | time is not the measure of truth | trust in your being

DAY 21:   A New Beginning   98
true meditation is not a separate activity | attune yourself | let go willingly | Love is incapable of asking for anything | use your reactions

WEEK 4:   The Seven Obstacles

DAY 22:   Losing Your Center   104
perspective changes | sense the senselessness | not stayed on this path | fear of change | unpreparedness | within your center | attune to truth | surety in God

DAY 23:   Believing in Unworthiness   108
not worth the effort | ridicule | badge of suffering | positive expectation | compliment yourself

DAY 24:   The Belief in Missing Out   110
           collecting disappointments | experiences | audacious
           behavior | life exists | somewhere other than with
           yourself

DAY 25:   The Fear of Loss of Control   112
           fears are illusory | addictions | compulsions | senses as a
           grounding point | self-destructive coping mechanisms |
           analyzing others | confess your fears | God know

DAY 26:   The Fear of Lack   116
           inner abundance which sustains | large appetites |
           voracity of feeding | sharing the self | a healthy
           responsibility

DAY 27:   The Voice of Self-Deprecation   120
           illusion of limitation | being nothing | your inabilities |
           hearing your true voice | recognizing your own nature

DAY 28:   Vulnerability to Judgment   122
           special authority | hyper-sensitivity | collects
           embarrassments | seen as | appearances | stand as who
           you are

Appendix A: References   125

Afterword

Acknowledgments

First, I am not able to adequately express the large amount of gratitude I hold towards the channels of A Course in Miracles, The Pathwork Guide Lectures, The Michael Teachings, and The Law of One: Helen Schucman, Eva Pierrakos, Sarah Chambers, and Carla Rueckert; as well as to those who have supported them all in their dedication to their calling. For bringing their transformative teachings to the world I offer my humblest thanks and appreciation: You've each helped make my own personal experience a whole lot more understandable and have provided me the means to find my own internal teacher.

In addition, my sincere thanks and appreciation goes out to my teachers Rupert Spira, Shunryū Suzuki, Jiddu Krishnamurti and Alan Watts, who, along with the above channeled teachings have greatly informed my own spiritual practice and inspired an enormous amount, if not all of this book: Thank you each for encouraging me to find my own spiritual practice and arming me with the appropriate tools to do so.

Any gems you find within the text of this book are most-assuredly theirs, and any errors I claim as mine in advance. I would encourage everyone to spend time familiarizing themselves with all these teachings, and when you feel called, to work with them in earnest practice.

Last, my thanks to my daughter Emily, for making such cute drawings for this book. It was great fun collaborating on this project! Em, you're a wonderful artist and a talented writer. Love you.

Preface

For as long as I can remember, I've always had a hunger for learning. I would absorb something and then apply that learning to a larger domain or context. Honestly, it makes sticking to one thing rather impossible. Unless some field of study is multifaceted and multilayered in its domain, I "check out" rather quickly. It started young, exploring universes, through cataloging every type of seashell, paper airplane, or musical instrument; every type of music, constellation, or dinosaur. When I found a new Lego brick, the Lego universe grew, and so did all the potential applications. When any universe stopped growing, I moved onto learning about the next. As I got older, I found that most every thought system I had encountered cyclically extended to new thought forms and then pruned the unused branches from itself. And so it continued, extending and pruning, extending and pruning.

The universe of spirituality has been unique for me, as the more I learned, the clearer the apparent unity and infinity of forms became. In time, the hunger to jump from form-to-form led to a singular content and context. A year ago, this culminated in the idea of metapaths, as the name for a style of learning and spiritual practice I've always felt called to. This book is a product of that recognition, a practice of meditative self-study inspired by my own, as informed by multiple teachings. Such a practice doesn't rely on only one teaching to guide, and so both the specialness and weakness of following any single form is balanced by seeking the unifying truths through our experience as pointed to by multiple forms. The metapath focuses on *you* being the key to your learning through applying the outer teachings to your inner world. In such a way, you are consistently reaffirmed as the pot which holds all the ingredients from which the stew is made. It is the practice then, which unifies.

Each chapter was written through a process of inner dictation during my own daily practice, arising as an inspired text, although it was not a strictly channeled text as the introduction and the afterword were. Admittedly, it somewhat wrote itself once I stepped aside. Daily, I may have set the intention, but the text arose from some other place within me. It came in the form of my internal teacher, or spirit guide. To that end, I am not the teacher, but simply another student of the universal curriculum, as imparted by this format. I had no preconceived goal, except to be as honest and open to receiving the voice as possible. This is the form it assumed on its own. After it was written, my eleven-year-old daughter, Emily, drew one adorable illustration per chapter to capture common themes.

At most, read one chapter a day and apply it in your daily life. Let it encourage and guide your own effort in living a more fulfilling life. Every four weeks, repeat the cycle, for as long as it feels relevant and useful. Other than that, there are no set rules. Like all tools, there is no single right way to use it. If this work inspires just one to look deeper into their being to what lay hidden in their own shadows, then it has fulfilled its intended purpose.

In the end, religion is about *you* and your relationship to the divine potential, as cast from divinity itself. Any other interpretation which includes a God outside you, a world outside you, or a savior outside you is in error.

Go in God. Be blessed.

Introduction

As unprepared as many in your species are to take the next step, we offer our understanding to this work with humility and everlasting praise to the AllOne, with the hope that our combined efforts help bring more of your people towards recognition of their true nature. It is only through honoring the singular joining within our density and polarity that such an offering can be made by us.

This work fulfills much of what we hope to be able to transmit to your people, within the context of the teach/learning device requested: a meditative cycle, which the practitioner can use as a guide towards the ongoing opening of their heart towards the AllOne. You may find this work challenging to understand, and many areas of it may contain terms which are new to you. We encourage you to postpone your judgment and simply perform the daily guidance as it appears. By doing so, the terms will become meaningful. We assure you of this. As well, we would like to provide our assurances that nothing within could be considered supernatural or mystical for its own sake. We urge you to leave your superstitions at the door, or at the most use your own reaction to them on your journey to learn more about yourself. As with all temporary thought systems they serve a purpose until they are laid down naturally by the thinker. Your identity is no different, and neither is ours. We could be seen as slightly ahead of where you are and be regarded as a big brother who cares about making the most of your efforts on your journey. Your planet will make the transition when it is right. They who have done so will rejoice, not out of a sense of compulsion or urgency, but out of a freedom to express their truest being.

You will find the layout of this book cyclic in nature and holographic in its symbolism. All words that are used can be interchanged with whatever words make more sense to you. It is the content under the words which we wish to impart. We believe, with an open heart, you will be able to find this. The content is available to the depth that you wish to find it. This is the best we can do in speaking of the truth. We urge you not only to study the words of this book but to use it in a practice that's ever evolving towards our shared, singular, unified nature, and in honor of it. We have done our best to ensure that only that which is constructive has been imparted in the writing of this work. Still, whatever does not resonate with you, you may pass by.

It is designed to be used in a four-week cycle, and continuously repeated, for as long as it holds purpose. Each time around the cycle further unfoldment will occur. Take the time to make it your own but limit yourself to one chapter per day maximum. You may put this book down whenever you want but the curriculum will live on in you, as it lives on in us. Those who find us will find it. And those that will find other means to address the curriculum will as well. There are infinite ways you each have found, and will continue to find, to express your true self more genuinely: this guidance is simply one of them. Never forget to laugh, whatever your chosen path.

We thank you for your efforts with deepest gratitude toward our unified nature in our singular Source. And we wish you the greatest of fruit in your own practice. Whatever is done, enjoy the journey.

We send you blessings from the AllOne.

(channeled February 18, 2022)

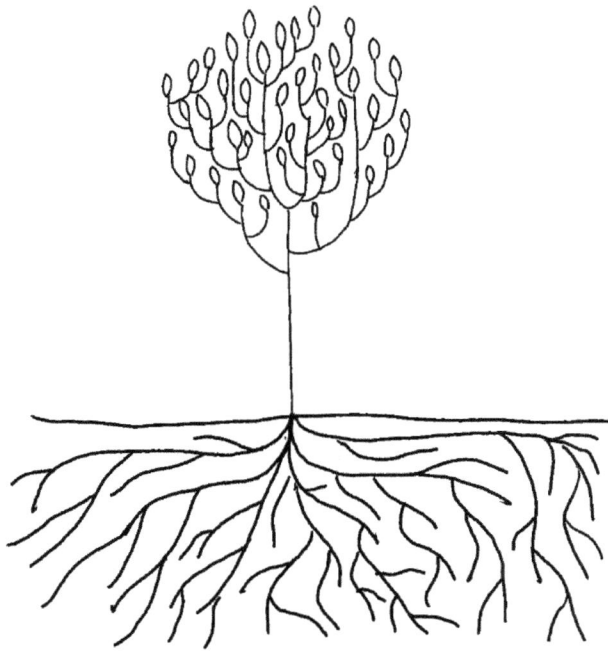

WEEK 1:
Core Practice

Day One
Direct Observing Within

For today, simply practice returning your attention to being aware, and investigate the nature of that awareness.

You can neither take yourself to a place you don't exist, nor to a time which is not now.

Are you aware?

You quickly say yes out of habit or belief, but for today, try this. Let go of your belief and simply pause and deliberately check. Direct your attention to your awareness and confirm this based solely on your own experience. Are you **aware**? Do not check if you are aware of this or that situation, or aware of an idea or a concept, or aware of your body's sensations, the passage of time, or even your feelings. Simply, are you aware?

Notice how you confirmed this, and do it again, watching the confirmation process as well. For a moment simply **direct your attention** to your awareness. Do not just read these words. Go, attempt to look on it like it were a painting. You are aware that you are aware. You know you are aware. And you know because you are certain. There is no question about it.

Try once more. Check your awareness again, and this time go a bit further by closing your eyes and spend several moments watching your thoughts or emotions rise and fall away. Welcome them as you direct your attention briefly to them. You know they come and go because they change over time. While some emotional or mental states may last longer than others, they are all temporary. This, you can sense yourself.

Throughout the day, look for any transience in your awareness itself. You may notice that your attention towards awareness, or your *awareness-of-awareness*, changes over time, but your awareness itself does not come and go. It remains ever-present, and it is changeless because awareness does not change over time. You cannot have an experience of no awareness. And you can verify this because it is known by you. In fact, you know it so well that you may easily take it for granted and not recognize its power.

It is not possible to experience thoughts, perceptions, or emotions and body sensations without awareness. You've spent much of your waking life directing your attention to **objects of experience** and not to the subject itself: **self as I**, also known as awareness. You willingly choose to shine the very light of awareness onto a myriad of objects, be they thoughts, perceptions, or emotions and body sensations, and willingly choose to overlook that which is shining within.

Now, what is I? Is it your own changing **context** informing your personal collections of thoughts, perceptions, and emotions and body sensations? Or is it testified by your own ideas about your history, your story or your drama as informed by your personal **relationships**? Or perhaps it is encapsulated in all your **achievements** and desires in this life, about your family, your career, your possessions, or your experiences? Maybe it is reflected in your ideas about the **structures** of country, customs, culture, religion, profession, study, party, family, race, gender, or age? Or perhaps it arises for you simply based on evolutionary **survival**?

Although each of you habitually **focus** on one area above, none of these experiences can encapsulate or define your true nature as awareness, and you know this as well. Whatever objects preoccupy your mind with the **concepts** of I, the concepts of I are simply just that: concepts. And concepts are not awareness. Concepts are objects clothing awareness. Yet, like all objects, they also must always arise within it, made of it. The self as I is not an object. It can observe, yet never be observed as an object of itself. This is **God**.

I Am. God is. What is the nature of God? Well, what is the nature of your awareness? Check it for yourself. You know it inherently, regardless of the concepts and stories your culture overlays onto it. You've witnessed to it above, and I'm certain you can witness to it again in an instant. This is not supernatural. In fact, it would be unnatural if you couldn't. You hear God through me, as I Am. I speak through you as I Am. You are God's activity and host.

You observe and respond to your **observations** through thought as a willful activity. Your will is always informed by your present thought, your present perception, or your present emotion and body sensation. The amount each informs your decisions is unique to your incarnated experience and varies due to many things, including the type of circumstance you are observing.

Your thoughts about the past are simply thoughts, and they are present now. In fact, all thought rises and falls in the present. Today, you can observe this. Any object, regardless of what it is, **receives life** through your awareness, which is ever-present *now*. This, you also can observe quite easily. The life given to a memory must be given by you today, or else that memory ceases to exist. You can make alive today *anything* you choose to focus your attention on, be they thoughts, perceptions, or emotions and body sensations. *You* are the dreamer of dreams.

The same is true of your thoughts about other locations. Even as you think on them or people at a great physical distance, your awareness is always ever-present *here*. In fact, there is nowhere else, and your connection to the other often testifies to it. A common mistake is to sense awareness within your body and attach to it there. For almost all of you, this belief is so strong you fear loss of your body upon bodily death. There is nothing to truly fear. You can neither take yourself to a place you don't exist, nor to a time which is not now. No one takes you anywhere at bodily death. You simply lay down your bodily *activity*.

Be assured today, whether you recognize it or not, you will always choose based simply on what you want to experience, for in your choice, so will be your experience. Life in spirit is ever moving, ever dynamic. Attend to what you **will** to strengthen in your mind. Everything is permissible. And it will bring experiences informed by the spirit it is sought with. It must, for you always **abide in self**, in God, in I Am.

Know thyself as you are. All objects arise for you, today and always, to potentially experience yourself in relation to them. Your present personality is one such object and activity, which you will lay down one day. In time, all will testify to one context. Today, to renew your own intent, simply state, *"Above all else, I want to see."*

I Am always here, whenever you decide to notice our journey together. Go with a beginner's mind, open and willing to see anew. For today, simply practice returning your attention to being aware, and investigate the nature of that awareness. And whenever you find yourself lost in an object, return to this simple practice of finding **God within**.

Day Two
Working Without

Today, the outer work is a calling to live this awareness within the activities and circumstances of life. Investigate the nature of your thoughts, your perceptions, and your emotions and body sensations, knowing they are initially interpreted based on your own past experiences.

Today, you embrace life.
You observe I Am within the myriad of forms.

Once you see I Am for what it is, for what you are, your awareness-of-awareness is awakened. And each time you spend time within a state of recognition of I Am, centered on your presence as infinite awareness, you gain a bit more understanding of the nature or **attributes of unitive consciousness** in your own recognition. Patience would speak to you of your ability to see each color of it slowly unfolding through your own consistent practice, cycle after cycle.

I Am is not a *state* of consciousness; it is consciousness itself. Initially, even the experienced momentary state is sometimes experienced as timeless. Timelessness is not only one of its attributes, but it is also your complete nature. Each attribute of your core being contains the whole of it, and so each attribute doesn't obstruct or block any other attribute. Nor can each true attribute be only a part of the pie, else you could cut I Am into pieces. In essence, within each attribute is the whole.

Each attribute is a **filter** which you are seeing I Am through. And each time you go within today, you may appreciate I Am with a new filter, or a specific way of looking within. Yet, within your own human experience, the inner work, the recognition of the nature of I Am is still only the first step. In time, you seek the next step once you notice the disconnect between your **inner and outer** lives. It will then feel more appropriate to move into a deeper expression of this recognition in the outer world. As within, so without.

After each time you **meditate**, you experience having to return to the outer world; there is no surprise there. And at first the clear light of your own being in a meditative state is most often received in a momentary, instantaneous flash of recognition, and experienced when you are willfully still from activity. The injunction, *"Be still and know I Am,"* is not specifically a request to go into a sitting meditative activity. This **stillness** always is, and can be accessed anywhere, at any time, no matter what activity you happen to be engaged in. Notice this today. It is here now.

Initially, recognition of this stillness is almost always sought within a state where you limit activity, to focus your attention inward to I Am. Yet, as you engage in your own practice, deeper with every cycle, you see that the attributes of I Am are not limited to any specific space or boundary including your body. I Am is unlimited, and it calls you to witness to it not only within you, but also working within the world and the other which all appears quite plainly outside of you. They aren't. This challenges how you relate to both what appears outside you, and how you relate to what appears within, as private thoughts.

The nature of the outside world or other can be explored as objects of perception and sensation, or in other words, how the outside world impinges on your inner world. You can observe this when completing your meditation activity today. Suddenly this results in a growing number of objects impinging on *you*. While you may initially feel calm or centered after your meditative activity, you experience a come down, back to what you consider to be the real world, much of which is habitual.

Returning to activity may be experienced as being caught once again by the objects of the world, which are still steeped in the **duality** of self/other, us/them, past/future, left/right, up/down, black/white, in/out, either/or, all/nothing, right/wrong. In the early cycles, the outer world still seems to affect the inner world, because your capacity to recenter appears reduced. You may even picture the act of meditation as going to I Am, when you really don't go anywhere. You may also exclude the outer world on purpose.

In some manner, you find it helpful to **limit your outer activity** while you meditate. But a practice of momentary recognition of your true being, one which is accessed only through limiting your activity, must be as limited as your living. Therefore, at first, you may experience this as a time of doubt or frustration, or of limited progress, wasted efforts, or stagnation. Your doubts scream:

> *"What's all this meditation for anyway? It's only a trick, an illusion, that I can shut off the real world. See? It always comes back. It's not worth the effort."*

I know you can recall the frustration of living in such a trap, especially when you have cyclically returned to your practice after falling off it, repeatedly. Yet, *any* disturbance is an opportunity for the deepening of self-facing, which always leads towards self-abidance. The call you are making to yourself is your **prayerful intent**, and you *are* worth the effort.

Today, in keeping separate any single part within you, you will inevitably keep separate a part of what seems to lie outside of you. As within, so without. Thus, it is essential that the kingdom that is initially found within, must as well be inhabited in potentially all your worldly activities for it to come to manifest the fullness that it is. And when you are called in this way, you naturally add another approach to your practice, which we focus on today.

Yesterday, with the **inner work**, you first investigated the nature of your being by a process of sensing the objects that you are *not*: thoughts, perceptions, and emotions and body sensations. This was not to deny the reality of your experiences in the inner and outer worlds, in as much as it was to gain a momentary vision of that which exists unchanged throughout all experience: I Am. And while I Am is no thing, it can be visualized conceptually as the screen upon which all things take their shape and have their existence in the movie of space-time experience which arises only on the screen. I Am is both everything and nothing, as its nature gives rise to every thing, and yet is no thing in itself.

Today, the **outer work** is a calling to live this awareness within the activities and circumstances of life. Such a calling urges you to investigate each of the objects you encounter while remaining in your center. You do not need to leave your center to do this activity. Simply investigate the nature of your thoughts, your perceptions, and your emotions and body sensations, knowing they are initially interpreted based on your own past experiences. From this, the layers of conditioning are seen less purposeful, let go of willingly, and the outward life becomes more infused with the true self. God can be not only *found*, but also *walked with*. The *path to God* must inevitably turn to the *path in God*.

Once you are ready to truly look, the inner work immediately awakens you to the presence of I Am. The outer work we focus on today is not so immediate, nor experienced as revelatory. You truly work *at it*. It may take lifetimes. It is experienced as never complete. Presently, your greatest blessing is that you have a lifetime of activity to draw from, and a large array of lenses through which to gain awareness of the self as manifesting as the union of all things, with all of life. Note, the Lord's Prayer starts with the words *Our* Father, not *My* Father.

Of course, you may choose to attend to it diligently, or not. The timing for this work is not fixed, though the lessons are essential and *will* be completed by you, for you are the host, and your life is the present lesson. Feel free to ignore this work *if that is what appears good and right* in each moment. *Nothing* is benefitted by forcing what you think are the lessons. An open heart is one which is present with how things are, not how they should be. Yet, this external activity is simply an out-picturing of your internal recognition and acceptance of the lifeforce. So, what is initially seen as a great effort or sacrifice, is fully realized as little or no effort, because it is what you want.

Within today's practice is the very joy of being, as experienced in activity. You learn a process, which in time, helps you to fully see and confront your **obstacles**, acknowledging them in all their distortion and darkness, and learn to release them in Love to the ever moving, ever present lifeforce. This universe is the experience of **movement**, of change over time. Only by unearthing that which lies within your deepest shadow can you love yourself as you are and be free to move in the flow of life.

Today, you embrace life. You observe I Am within the myriad of forms. Over cycles, you learn that your mistakes made from your own freewill are precisely what make it possible for you, and everyone, to find another way. Human injustice gives rise to divine justice through the spiritual laws. For the outer work today, you may find it easiest to initially work with objects which appear to originate from outside your body and personality: perceptions and sensations, especially in early cycles. In later cycles, the more interior objects of emotions and thoughts can be added to this, the outer work.

Perception is how you *see* the outside world, or the image you hold of it. **Sensation** is how you sense your body's interaction with it. You can add this outer focus onto your practice today easily, after about five or ten minutes of inner work. Look fully towards a sensation you feel within a part of your body and note the feeling within your breath, perhaps first on your lips or nasal passages. Bring the sensation towards you as you focus your attention on it. Maintaining your center, in an unhurried manner feel what it must be to fly through this sensation as you would a cloud. Where is its edge? Does it have a border at all? Here, you are as an infant, so the ideas you have held of what your body is cannot distort your experience of the sensation. If time permits and no sense of strain is felt, try another sensation. In later cycles, try more painful experiences, all while staying centered in I Am unthreatened.

When it feels right, perform this work with your **perceptions** of a given event or circumstance. Consider a specific place or person to bring this event closer to your center. Again, sense what objects of perception arise. Be patient with yourself. For some, this can take quite a long time to notice, and for others it is so immediate it appears quite unstable. Simply acknowledge what does arise, when it does, and if you lose your center and chase an object of perception, go back to the inner work of yesterday. If you find yourself wrapped up in an emotion or thought, again, go back to the inner work. Soak your dirty cloth in the water, and in time the dirt will present itself to be liberated without scrubbing.

The perception may say to you, and sometimes in quite a loud voice, *"Come here... go down this road with me."* Rather than following it down that road today, ask it, in Love, to tell you about the road, while you remain centered in I Am. You'll find the courage in innocence to earnestly say to your perceptions:

> *"Come over for a visit and let's have a chat. You can stay for as long as you'd like. You're loved and accepted here. I won't ask you to leave once I've fulfilled my obligation."*

By doing this, you will start to set up a willingness to receive your own perceptions as they arise each cycle, be they accurate or inaccurate. In time, you will start to simply love them for what they are. This opens the door to vision. Today, to renew your own intent, simply state, *"Above all else, I want to see."*

Vision becomes clearer as one experiences the nature of the objects of perception, be they accurate or inaccurate. An accurate perception is initially *that which agrees with your beliefs* and an inaccurate one is *that which is out of agreement*, because initially, the purpose of your perception is directed towards your own aim as a separate personality based on your separate identity.

While focusing on survival, structure, achievement, and early relationships this self-agreement can be an extremely useful tool with which you build your *independence* within this world. But as a mature adult who tries to work within the context of developing and maintaining loving relationships, when you buy into it as more than just a tool, you aggrandize the self, and you incorrectly invest your being into this agreement and lose the context of its utility. By seeing this, you can begin to open to the idea that an accurate perception is that which simply fulfills your **purpose**, be it in or out of agreement with your present beliefs.

When your purpose is to live more genuinely within I Am, to walk with God, you can more easily admit, *"Everything I perceive, I see it as I have made purpose for."* You recognize that *nothing* gets around your perception. *Everything* you interact with fulfills your purpose. You may wrestle with this recognition for many lifetimes. But be assured you will always remain true to who you believe you are, even if you momentarily like to pretend that you're less. And indeed, you all do like to pretend. It is fun.

Your work in prior cycles may help you see that your perceptions can arise from false beliefs, such as a scarcity of Love, a malevolence in the nature of God or others, or feeling weak or little in a powerful world. And as you progress further, you will recognize that these false beliefs gave these perceptions their purpose at that time. Yet, all objects serve the purpose of the perceiver. As a perceiver, you can *always* **choose again**. Affirm this today. You can choose healing, integration, and self-facing. As you begin to ask more earnestly, you start seeing God as I Am infused within all things, enlivening them with unifying attributes of innocence, strength, and benevolence. You become an extension of that inner power. The activity of the world becomes a dance of creation rather than a projection of fear.

Then vision has arrived. It may seem to leave you momentarily, but it will never be forgotten. You will still play within a world of inaccurate perceptions; of that be reassured. Yet, a new day has dawned. You know it is play, and not so serious. The innocent perception as accurate perception has arrived. *"Father, forgive them, for they know not what they do,"* is applied within you, not just in the external world. You can thus say, *"I see I was mistaken and I'm learning to be open to life, to love myself and others."*

And so, in time, judgment is laid down, as it was never your true nature.

Day Three
Illusion and the Ego Dance

Today, make it a point to ask for guidance wherever you mistake yourself for an ego. In doing so, you learn to rely on a broader context than your ego activity can ever conceive of.

Your inner gold is always infinitely valuable without anyone claiming they agree with its value.

Ego activity is informed by the belief in limits as superimposed on your spirit. You may not notice it, but you are directing your awareness so quickly to your own **belief in ego needs** that you almost don't need me to point them out in the first place. In later cycles, you'll see that less is more. Today, you'll work on what seems to stand in the way of embracing the fuller shift to recognition of my voice. *Nothing* stands in the way, except your own belief that something does, and your belief that you cannot live fully without that thing in some way. It's actually the other way around: you haven't fully lived ever with that thing, for it requires effort to maintain its protection.

You may like the idea of sharing new recognitions of the ego with significant others and seeing if you get positive feedback from their ego. While it makes you happy to receive agreement from a loved one, it's time to see what lies behind it. You put a lot of effort in assuming detailed motivations of others underneath the dynamics observed, and this only serves to further entangle your ego into your own perception of other's mess, all the while maintaining your own mess. The act of alertness to the dynamics of another's ego must always utilize your ego, for by doing so you project and teach separation, which rests on limits. The only thing required of you is to accept your true nature for yourself, wholly. Everything else, including **ego analysis** is a product of your own ego dynamics.

First, let us reassure you, it's not bad to do the ego dance. It's time though for you to see how much it exists all throughout every nuance of your life. And the nicer forms of it are equally destructive to your peace. All forms of illusion are total. There are no greater or lesser illusions just as there are no expressions of Love that are more difficult than any other. All are maximal. Though without your **belief in illusions**, they are nothing. Yet with your belief, even the apparently nicest forms of them block unity, love, and joy from unfolding.

You fool yourself by over-focusing on your more obvious faults, so that you overlook or even praise their apparent lesser forms thinking they're innocuous or even a virtue! No illusion is powerless, with your belief. And when one illusion truly leaves, so must all. Thus, any progress in what you claim as partial healing is just illusion as well, only a shell game to hide your illusions in forms under nicer rocks you won't turn over to see their existence staring at you.

In a very real sense, **incremental healing** is not progress at all. It is simply a longer path, or a delay to healing. When you get lost in the smaller gradations, you lose the awareness of the nature of belief in illusion being total. You also lose the awareness of the nature of healing, which is, as well, total. In an instant sight comes. In an instant it is all lost sight of. Deception is complete, or not at all. There are no unique levels which hold a different purpose.

Today, you are calling yourself to see your own deviations from truth in the light of truth, to inspire the only fitting response to yourself and your brother: **appreciation and forgiveness**. This is the act of laying down the weapon of all evaluation, all analysis of the self and the other in the process. Use evaluation for what it is meant for, to see the true from the illusory substitute. You must see that you cannot educate your ego away, judge it, or even change it by force. These acts strengthen a new form of it to arise, perhaps under a different name or claim, for the ego is merely a mistaken activity of the self.

Ego activity is simply **incremental activity**. You're so used to learning incrementally that you don't trust the instantaneous I Am, the holy instant, for being the true manifestation of all that you are. If you did, you'd see that it holds the truest treasures immediately experienced. *Today*, you can simply choose to place your ego in the service of the spirit of wholeness who accepts all your illusions as they are. Along with your higher self, the spirit of wholeness, or *Holy Spirit*, uses them to improve your ability to recognize your error in holding a purpose of separation. When this is truly seen, they will be laid down without any show or comment.

With each repeated cycle, you're so close to walking into this new area of practice willingly. The doorknob is right near your hand, we assure you. In fact, it takes effort to stay where you are, in stagnation. It will be the greatest relief to let it go and find your own self full and ready to be shared with all you feel called to do so with. You'll literally laugh in a crazy laugh how seemingly foolish it was to trade this fullness of self for the idols you hold onto: agreement on one's analysis of ego dynamics. It's like trading **your gold** for another's **paper currency**. You already know it's worthless without their buy in. Yet your inner gold is always infinitely valuable without anyone claiming they agree with its value.

The conditioning is held in place by an idea of you being dependent on circumstance or on another for your very being.

You're not. And this you will see today. What you may also notice is quite the opposite: that in the worst situations the calmness and security of your pure being radiates without much work. Any effort to make yourself ready or prepare the way for an act of Love, pushes the expression of that Love further away in time from your giving and receiving it. You **need not prepare** or make yourself ready. The gift of I Am is always present to receive. Today, let everything else drop.

A spiritual practice does not work to make you ready; it simply allows you to do what you wouldn't choose to discipline yourself to do otherwise. It gives you a chance to experience a new dynamic, to see the evidence even if you continue to stumble. It's natural to persist in wanting the old security blankets. A lot of this you **understand with your intellect**, yet you'll choose to not acknowledge it in your choices for quite some time. Today, never forget to laugh as you notice what initially appears as insanity from within you.

Laughter of **release** can unify the self as easily as tears of release can. Today you can release from the ego structures as you seem to join with I Am anew. In your meditation, the seeing of peace first arises within you, and then extends outward, just as seeing conflict starts within and is then projected outward. Extension creates like itself as Love inspires it. The ego projects in its attempt to perceive a world which is so unlike you, and in early cycles you are *almost always* in ego activity without recognizing it.

Today, make it a point to *ask* for guidance wherever you mistake yourself for an ego. In doing so, you learn to rely on a broader context than your ego activity can *ever* conceive of. This is useful because your conceptions have brought you to a place of *needing another way*. Today you choose to lay the ego down by **admitting you don't know**. Why else would you need a guide? Would you rather be right or happy? A new beginning comes again today when you pray within:

> *"Today I lay down all my evaluations and I give You my perceptions to reorient towards truth. I choose simply to be open, to receive the good, no matter in what form it may seem to appear. I Am available to extend Your presence, which is always available. Whenever I sense separate ownership arising, I will lay down my own thoughts throughout the day in laughter and ask for guidance."*

Day Four
Invention

Today, you will take time to see that all concepts are ego ideas. You will work with everything that arises in your perception, throughout your day, as your inventions, either making distortions or creating by extending the lifeforce.

While what you see is of your own making,
you can always choose creative vision in I Am.

You have invented **the world you see**; of this you can be sure. In all its aspects, whether they appear positive or negative, informed by limitation or abundance; ridicule or acceptance; condemnation or forgiveness; malevolence or beneficence; be certain you've invented this. The world you see is a world distorted by illusion. And in a tragic choice such as this, does it make any difference if you see yourself as the victim or the hero?

Healthy, positive human love is an invention in I Am, as an extension of Love. It matters only what you want to see. And so, while what you see is of your own making, you can always choose **creative vision** in I Am. This is what today is for.

All objects of perception are *inventions* in perception. In other words, you make how you see. And all circumstances and situations you see may be classified within one of four categories: the inner and outer distorted world; and the inner and outer loving world. The first two categories contain distorted perceptions, and both can be based in either **grasping or aversion**. Grasping affirms you want more of something, which appears limited. Aversion affirms a disturbance in a form of pain or suffering, a component of which appears larger than your own limited ability to tolerate it. The last two categories contain loving perceptions and do not hold the same pleasure/pain or desire/aversion duality, as all in Love is in joy.

Joy is experienced as a deeper, truer pleasure of creating new life because it is an application of the divine lifeforce. There is not a living thing which has not experienced it. As children, you felt such joy in the nurturing from your parents. As teens, you felt it in the independence of the freedom you learned to express. As adults, you've encountered this same dynamic in sex when it is engaged creatively, resulting in a bonding of souls and a full open giving of your abundance to another intimately. Joy always creates like itself.

Unlike the imbalanced see-saw of duality which occurs in distorted perception arising out of the ego's belief in limitation, in the loving world you see the balance inherent in the trinity, or the **triune nature** of our creation:

1. Inspiration/Emotion
2. Expression/Thought
3. Action/Will

Since the distorted world must still arise in I Am, the distorted echoes of the triune nature of divinity are also present in manifestations of distorted perception but seen through the lens of illusion. In other words, you cannot leave Love, no matter how deeply you believe you have. And while you cannot make perfect polarity, you can believe you have, and you will act accordingly. Today, you will take time to see that *all concepts* are ego ideas. And like all ego ideas, they can be useful, as **concepts have a use** to the Holy Spirit in healing your belief in the separation.

The concept of the trinity must also arise in the **ego's framework**. You can see this simply by how fast you can shift the three balanced components of thought, emotion, and will into *positive* ideas of truth, love, and courage, as well as *negative* ideas of pride, fear, and self-will. Anywhere the limited concepts of positive and negative are overlaid onto objects, you observe evidence of ego-thinking clouding the demonstration of Love in truth.

For today, work with everything that arises in your perception, throughout your day, as your inventions, either making distortions or creating by extending the lifeforce. Stay as attentive as you can, without forcing yourself. You will notice in later cycles that *every relationship* of which you are a part has elements which are truly **holy** and therefore in whole Love. Distortions of **specialness** may persist, especially in early cycles, but won't persist for long. In time, all *loving aspects* will arise clearly in your perception.

For today, you may find it convenient to bin some of your relationships as *special-love* but it would do you well to admit that this limited all-or-nothing categorization is an oversimplification. Your relationships aren't only special or holy but have components of both. Even if the energies arising in them are informed by a strong component of grasping or averting, know that Love lies within and can always inform holiness. And what two truly share takes nothing away from others, as it is shared with all in full openness.

As you practice today, giving your meditative awareness to your perceptions, you *will* notice more **aspects** in every relationship where you have testified to Love and have answered the call of your true nature, be it with friends, family, coworkers, or acquaintances. Every aspect of true relationship is ultimately in truth and holiness. For now, every ego relationship seems to hold some truth and many illusions. In later cycles, the illusions are let go of willingly, through Love as acceptance. In the end, illusion is never experienced in Love.

As only illusions are weak, Love cannot ever be threatened and so requires no defense. Let today be the day you see the Love in personal creation.

Day Five
Strength and Vision

When you choose without God's vision then something of your own making stands in the gap between His vision and yours, because you alone believe fully in what you alone make. Today you will see that whenever you choose to believe in an object of your own making, you always have the choice to choose again.

Consciousness must be emanating from Source filled with lifeforce, just as the leaf is always connected to the tree and would be lifeless without it.

Vision and strength must be one as without vision, strength is unseen and unknown. Without strength, vision is unstable. Both seemingly go out into a world of perception, or within to an interior world. The focus of strength and vision on the exterior world, to decide anything, is a substitute for your reality. The focus of strength and vision on the interior world provides you operate out of your own **true nature**, thus honoring your presence, which always results in true inner peace. All strength is of God as I Am, as is all vision. There are *no* exceptions. Strength and vision are singular in the triune nature of I Am on the action/activity axis and are called *will* and *perception*. As we've stated yesterday, the triune nature is made up of will, thought, and emotion within you, cast from the domains of action, expression, and inspiration respectively.

The trinity is the balanced way of life. In fact, it is life itself expressed as the balance of divine attributes within you. Some of the **highest forms** on the will/action axis could be called courage, strength, vision, and true perception. Some of the highest forms on the thought/expression axis could be called truth, wisdom, and the word. Some of the highest forms on the inspiration/ emotion axis could be called love, innocent and positive intention, and joy. Today we focus on the will/vision axis which comes into form as both inner and outer activity.

You choose with God, or you do not choose with the strength of I Am within you, without God's vision. When you choose without God's vision then something of your own making stands in the gap between His vision and yours, because you alone believe fully in what you alone make. This thing you made is not real, yet it blocks His sight for so long as you believe it can. Let the idea fade which blocks you and sight you do have. **Remove the block**, and strength is felt. You can do it in an instant. Such an object seems to take strength away from you without your noticing, or rather, it appears to remove your choice to be strong as you are. How can you know? Simply remove it, and you will find the light of life shining to draw all strength from, uncorrupted and incorruptible.

Today you will see that whenever you choose to believe in an object of your own making, you always have the choice to choose again. This *is* the way to allow true vision and my voice to be heard within you, as your **higher self**, through what we've introduced as the spirit of wholeness, or the Holy Spirit. You can see the Holy

Spirit as the very basis, or DNA, of what *makes* the tree of consciousness possible in the myriad of forms it has. It unifies each and every leaf and branch on the tree as the code resides in every location of this tree as one component of God in the trinity, just as DNA does in biological life. I Am your higher self, my voice being your own vision back down your own branch, or a little further along in your reunification/soul evolution. I Am able to access more consistent *vision* at my density. Together with many spirits, we guide you. Yet all vision you experience comes by power of the code from the lifeforce flowing through me to you regardless of whether you know you are receiving it through me at any given time. On the **evolutionary tree** of unified consciousness, the trunk could be seen as the **Father**, or source of all life; the **Son**, or you and all creation, as all the branches and leaves; the **Holy Spirit**, or the code, as the inner spirit or DNA which we all share in one vision.

When in illusion, many of the leaves and even some branches can mistakenly not see their connection to each other, and some call this condition hell. It is not eternal, for nothing seemingly separate can be outside of time, as time was made by separation and limits. Yet when I Am is seen, the vision of the unified code is His *gift*, the vision of the Holy Spirit, as unity or **heaven**. The activity of the ego of singularly struggling for light and nourishment on its own is relinquished by the leaf and it embraces the unified activity of all life through the code emanating from Source as witnessed in all life. Consciousness must be emanating from Source filled with lifeforce, just as the leaf is always connected to the tree and would be lifeless without it. You can always choose to ignore that connection and believe in it, as the author or source of ego, but by your *unbelief* you cannot make your true self *untrue*. Unbelief in truth gives rise to the aspects of the **lower self** within the Son as the son of man, as *creation* is turned into simple *making*, uninspired by the Holy Spirit; the Father as will unseen and thus inactivated; and the word unexpressed. By the word, we do not mean your Bible, but rather the seed of form in every creation, the Sun or Logos expressed.

I always speak but sometimes you cannot hear by choice, listening as you do to your lower self, a voice which speaks loudly and with fear. Yet you are all connected to the branch, as fragments of your entity, and then to your soul tree, and to all souls evolving within their own entities. Yes, you are connected to that friend of yours, or that loved one, but you're presently blind to it more often than not. And within that blindness does life become uninspired, unexpressed, and inactivated. What replaces it is fear, pride, and self-will on those same three axes: love replaced by fear, truth replaced by ego-pride, will/strength/vision replaced by self-will and projection. As we said, the voice of your lower self speaks loudly. Today we simply acknowledge this.

You will not consistently hear my voice until you love yourself and **integrate the shadow** aspects of your lower self in Love. Its weakness is demonstrated by its insistence, defensiveness, unacknowledged uncertainty, joylessness, negativity, and its frantic shifting between urgency and sloth. Watch yourself today honestly to see such behaviors, and do not judge, simply accept them for what they are, with Love. Watch others to see such behaviors and accept them with Love as well. When in doubt, lovingly remind yourself that to forget yourself as being in God we must actively forget others as in God too. This type of outer work can take many, many cycles, as much of the obstructions are held in place by habitual patterns of misthought and have given rise to dense emotional energies held in the physical body. These take time to clear, even after you rationally see your mistake, therefore much is gained by being patient with yourself.

In later cycles, you'll sense the consistency and constancy of my voice. You'll know that no matter what your lower self insists on loudly, you can always sense my strong, secure presence and my voice **waiting patiently** for you to open to hear and receive the joy of I Am through a new voice of vision and strength. This is what a soul requires to develop while incarnated on this plane and helps you stay grounded for profitable soul work. One's vision is where one is *grounded*. One's strength is how a person *maintains* that ground/stability. Upon this, all loving action is based.

Presently, your **ego is decider**. So, when you make your own vision today, acknowledge that you do so from either ego alone or ego recognizing the presence of the Holy Spirit. The second opens the way for creation, as one gets more accustomed to *asking* for guidance. Strength will come proportionate to your *trust* in the answer. In the end *all strength* is of I Am, regardless of whether one recognizes or acknowledges it. Today, when you feel weak, know you have simply not chosen with I Am. Whenever you decide to choose again and give your thinking to Source, your pure awareness, thoughts will align coherently, truth will dawn, backed by a strength which dwarfs your own ego. Security and stability will be the first recognized attributes of such strength of true inner will. For today, your meditation is to attend throughout the day to which voice within you is your advisor helping you decide, based on the evidence of how you *feel*. Try to identify as many instances as possible, without feeling any burden. Patience would remind you that in subsequent cycles, more consistent attention can be paid with little increased effort.

Every day, every instant, you have that ability to **choose yet again** and become yourself, through *choosing to see your original nature for yourself*, and nothing matters apart from this. In later cycles, you will experience the ego dwarfing in your own meditation, the coming back home from accidentally chasing a spiraling trail of thoughts behaving like a monkey needing attention.

Today, you may indeed find it amazing to experience the power and the strength within, and how it takes over in the blink of an eye, making the monkey-chasing episode feel like a hazy dream. In the end, vision of all aligns to the true vision of self. At the very heart of it, *all* chasing of unreality *is* a hazy dream. All that's left as you awaken to truth is the Love, the Love we *share*, and the Love we *are*.

Day Six
Positive Intent in Action

Directing your attention to your actions doesn't mean forcibly altering your actions. But it does request you take some time to purposefully bless another today and to meditate on seeing that anything is possible in God, because you're not alone in making action happen.

It need not be perfect application as judged by the little ego-self.
It need only be perfect intent, which is positive, innocent, loving,
whole, utterly harmless, and utterly benevolent.

Today, we move ahead from inventing with positive intent at the level of *blessing* to **positive action** at the level of *doing*. Keep in mind that not all egoic expressions of external loving are always the loving positive action we wish to inspire in you, for example, nice, kind, sweet, passive, helpful, accommodating behavior or gestures. It is not the action itself which determines if it is loving or not. It is the *intent* or blessing that *lies behind* the loving action which makes it so. Not that perfection is needed today, no. But be easy on yourself if your ego says, *"You know you could step up and solve that problem for that person more than you do."* Taking control of others' situations is *not* loving in action because it may often be informed by fear, even if your ego tries to aggrandize it with pseudo-love. Allowing adults to be responsible and giving them time to feel the pain of shirking their own responsibilities may be the most appropriate and constructive loving action.

Remember, the pain in other's lives are a function of *their* seeing. And it is *never your work* to make another see. It is only your work to remove *your own blocks* to the awareness of love's presence. Therefore, the **appropriate loving activity** may be a variety of options, depending both on you, on them, and on what feels right to your blessing. Note, your blessing is infinite. Your doing is not, but ego activity may try to limit it even further. It's ok. Just be gently aware of this today as this is the first time *putting awareness of your own actions into your practice,* at least in the early cycles. Directing your attention to your actions doesn't mean forcibly *altering* your actions. But it does request you take some time to purposefully bless another today and to meditate on seeing that *anything* is possible in God, because you're not alone in making action happen. These are the keys behind a loving action based on truly loving intent. Whether you expect it will be noticed or not is not important and not constructive.

Herein lies your attempt to see into all action the breath of **infinite blessing**. It reaches far beyond where the little ego-self can operate; we promise you this. You are *not* alone. Let that sink in some. From here you go onward with an enormous power not of your making, which amplifies and orchestrates beyond your own ego awareness. In the morning, meditate on how your holiness unlocks the door to Love in action all around you. Extend this in action but a little today, and you'll see the amplification. You can be a vigilant witness to the amplification of fear underlying unloving activity, or of perfect intent underlying loving activity. It need not be perfect application as judged by the little ego-self. It need only be perfect intent, which is positive, innocent, loving, whole, utterly harmless, and utterly benevolent.

Be gently aware that even your most helpful ego activities can be informed partially with harmful or fearful intent in spirit. **Complete harmlessness** doesn't necessarily mean weak action if one feels called to act. It could be the strongest action or the strongest omission of action, but it will be filled with benevolence, appreciation, and gratitude. So, when you are projecting psychological pain in the situation of others, you make *your own* situation more painful by doing so. Then both you *and* that person will see themselves in error. Yet, when you pause and ask for guidance, there is nothing *your* holiness cannot do. Remember, it is only through *your* asking that you have the power to initiate. Don't transfer this to the need for others to see differently, for this is not your concern. Although all others are holy in God, *you* can access it only through *your* own holiness. We repeat ourselves, today, seeing for yourself your own original nature is *all* you must do.

Unloving thoughts are the **evidence of guilt**, even if it's not clear where guilt exists or why. Where and why aren't important here. Guilt keeps you in hell. Unloving thoughts remind you that you are holding guilt and are stuck in hell in this moment. Your holiness blesses you and saves you from guilt and saving yourself in this way *is* the answer to hold all in heaven, if indeed we are all Love and all One. From self-actualization comes self-realization. You're at the stem of the flower of positive intent. You've experienced the petals and the bud. Now feed it, and you will see your holiness *is* your salvation.

In later cycles, it will become clearer that we can *choose heaven* only by choosing peace for ourselves first. It naturally extends. There is nothing it cannot do. It blesses the world. It envelops everything we see. It manifests in a never-ending circle: sight, blessing, and activity, within the domains of thought, emotion, and will respectively. The highest form of thought is wisdom, the highest form of emotion is love, and the highest form of will is courage. **Claim your own** courage whenever fearful today, and move into holiness by saying:

> *"My holiness can courageously act by expressing salvation in thought, inspired by choosing to see Love within me."*

The circle becomes more complete and may be fully applied as Source, with I Am recognized within.

In the evening, reflect on how effective you felt in this activity through the day. At the very least, recognize that the blocks within you can now be called out without great defensiveness. In later cycles, your unloving thoughts about a person become clearer, so you can remove these blocks when ready as you grow beyond their original illusory purpose.

We will never attempt to **teach Love** to you for that is what you are. You are holy, and love is your inheritance and your salvation. In fact, it is heaven itself. Heaven is nowhere if not here and now and in you. That's where and when it *always* exists. Whether or not you see it, it is up to you to receive it when you truly want it. You can stay in hell for as long as you find purpose in it.

Day Seven
Living Truth

As you know, it is neither helpful nor healthy to consciously push away the lower self, nor to bask in its dynamics out of ignorance. What is helpful is how consistently you call on the context of the higher self when living with the lower self, and this is what we will do today. For today, know you are exactly where you're supposed to be.

Today, in your meditation, reflect on the idea that no matter who you believe you are and where you point, the living truth is in you.

We end your first week with a day of rest to reflect on the goodness you've embarked upon, inspired by what shines in you. Anyone who has been on a spiritual path of self-discovery and has seen truly but once has **awakened to truth** as much as an incarnated person could. Truth is something you always live with and live as, whether you see it or not. And as you are always welcome here in heaven, let me help you choose courageously to pause your habitual seeing, to look together today at where you believe you truly are. To see is to see truly without deception or self-flattery, with the seeing truth applied. This is self-realization, which leads to awakening.

The phrase, *"You're in truth,"* is said by some as shorthand for being in a good mindset. Yet your **lifeforce is always truth** itself, or you wouldn't be alive. This is what you testify to passively in every breath, and actively whenever you meditate on the idea of God. Awakening is the change of state from not seeing to seeing, yet what is your sight? And even if you have seen, have you lived in this seeing consistently? When born, every incarnated soul loses some of their sight due to the nature of matter, and so all can benefit by putting in some effort to recognize where they may be blind to the truth.

Moments of awakening to that applied truth is what calls to you while living with the energy of the lower self. As you know, it is neither helpful nor healthy to consciously push away the lower self, nor to bask in its dynamics out of ignorance. What is helpful is how consistently you call on the **context of the higher self** when living with the lower self, and this is what we will do today.

At this stage you would be mistaken in thinking that the lower self goes away without attempting to remain in some form. That process of incremental walking within God is far longer than a lifetime for nearly all the separated sons and daughters of God. Yet the desire for more clarity is understandable and natural for the incarnated soul looking for greater peace. At your own physical death, at this stage of soul evolution, you will find that veil lifted temporarily until the next incarnation.

For today, know you are exactly where you're supposed to be. Your lower self is as much your guide as your higher self, though it can only be seen as such when wrapped in the context of the higher self. Thus, go today with God, and all is as it will be for truth to shine now. That is how walking is. Within **every step of the journey** the other shore is reached. With each step does the fullness of the journey arise within you. The awareness of Love's fullness is complete or not at all. It can only be full *now*, not tomorrow.

I will say this: although you are my worldly ancestor: Awake, my *child!* In some sense you are my child in spirit within God. In some sense I Am your offspring in the incarnated form. Awake now! Then, after you return to sleep, you will wake once again recalling what it means to have awoken. It is much greater than a flash, though for now a flash will do. It is closer to the truth than the outdated spiritual idea you hold of the self not yet awakened. You believe you are on an unreal road back from an unreal place. Only the premise need be questioned to awaken now. All else is unreal and habitual. And tomorrow's habits are unwritten.

How can I be your child in an incarnated sense and yet your elder in spirit? Maybe you see that this implies that I also am not fully aware of truth. Yet I go before you as an elder brother. Anyone incarnated behind the veil has a marked tendency to see others as overly awakened, and yet we're all evolving. There's no tomorrow-you in fact, even if it is helpful to see me as such. I Am simply you in a very real sense. I Am the furthest ahead you wish to acknowledge in yourself now. I Am your apparent potential.

I Am what you will be in an incarnated sense, and therefore I Am *your child* or offspring. Yet, as you are returning while going forward, I Am *your elder* and your access to all that flows from the one Father by means of the code. We all have the code to share in. I must see it for you to be able to see it, and nothing you see have I not. I have not seen all, yet I Am walking you home just as we are all **walking each other home**. Come to me when you want to point as directly towards truth as you can. Yet, drop it all, including me as a separate voice, for us to connect in a flash to the one Father. In that moment we all see all. We can, we do, and we will.

The future is the dance towards what has always been. Yet it is only accessed ever today. Today is always a starting point, even when it appears an ending. You're doing very well, we assure you. And there are no *shoulds* at all. Today, you simply acknowledge **where you see yourself** at. And that is key.

It will bloom like a flower. It has been, and it will continue. You know you have called many times to your higher self. Know that but once was enough to start an avalanche. You're watching it unfold, but mind you, this may or may not be the **first call** across all your lives. Most definitely, it isn't. But it may be the first call as your incarnated personality you presently believe you are. The call was the very reason you made the life agreement for those closest to you to find you here to remember I Am in self. And either way, near or far, know that you're part of the avalanche.

Your own testifying to Love also encourages others to let their own avalanche unfold, in time. It continues, and gains momentum. This is the time-based loving context for your work on this path upcoming. Of course, all vision originates from Source directly. So, like all external forms of teaching, they are just **fingers pointing** at the moon, as the saying goes. You can point at truth just the same. Neither yourself, nor your brother's personhood is the moon, but you are both pointing towards it. Today, in your meditation, reflect on the idea that no matter who you believe you are and where you point, the living truth is in you.

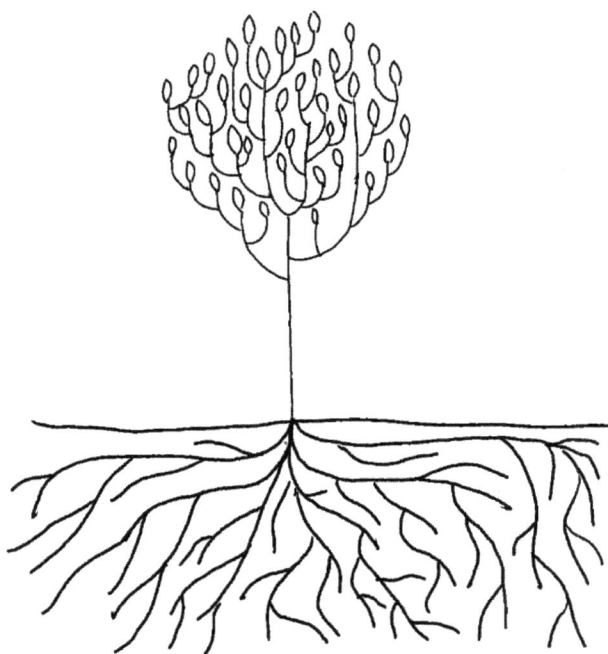

WEEK 2: Extension of Practice

Day Eight
Chasing Effects and Substitutes

If your practice maintains the proper focus, there is really nothing to be overly excited about. Go to the gold today, ready to receive, ready to share, and the secondary solitary pleasures will fade from purpose. If you search your heart, you will see that this has always been your experience on this path. The heart of communion is union.

The more you experience awareness-of-awareness the
less the highs are so overvalued. In time, the highs
give way to simple, peaceful self-abidance.

Our guidance not to chase the effects of meditation is built on the basic, clear idea that *awareness is not a state*. It is your eternal being. Yet **awareness-of-awareness** as a state *can* come and go. It may be fleeting in your practice and leave you thirsting for the next mountaintop experience. As such, it can be misused as an object which substitutes for your knowing of self-as-awareness. So, while awareness-of-awareness is useful to sense awareness, it is so easy to mistake it for the awareness you are. A good reminder whenever you reflect on the highs of awareness-of-awareness is that awareness itself is *nothing special*, because *everyone* is awareness *always*, even when not aware of it. If your practice maintains the proper focus, there is really nothing to be overly excited about.

Awakening is also **nothing special** in a supernatural or mystical sense, because its coming *is* the recognition of your natural state. That's not to say that the apparent reunification to God is not to be experienced as valuable in your walking this path. Yet, there comes a point where it becomes clear that the fleeting spiritual high just isn't what you're after. This may occur after many mistakes chasing the spiritual high, yet you start to notice the high fades quickly, and anything that fades *cannot* be your eternal being. The more you experience awareness-of-awareness the less the highs are so overvalued. In time, the highs give way to simple, peaceful self-abidance. Awareness-of-awareness becomes what it always was: a state where awareness is honored in self.

Even the lower self begins to serve the purpose of the Holy Spirit. All your missteps map out the lay of the land, including the experiences which don't work. But the spiritual law of **freewill** means as well that the solution must come by the same mechanism as the suffering: free choice. Human injustice leads to divine justice, and divine perfection comes through a long history of human imperfection. This relies on the running of all possible experiments much like your present view of how biological evolution functions. To eliminate freedom by having a superior power push truth on you breaks the spiritual law, which is impossible, for these laws which gave rise to the laws of your universe are even more firm and without remainder than your scientific approximations. Freewill: to you, it's both a bellyache and a blessing. The prodigal son says, *"Enough is enough!"* and Dorothy leaves Oz willfully, knowing home is where she can always be in an instant. It's just like when you wake to yourself, you exclaim, *"Enough playtime pretending I'm not what I Am! Enough roleplay!"* Then it's time to know thyself.

Being a point of least resistance, it's also why hallucinogens as a means to receive divine revelation through heightened yet solitary experience cannot be effective long term. They illuminate but once or twice because they **dampen your ability to experience** the gravity or weight of freewill and communion. Without applying this perspective, the experience of the high itself becomes an idol of diminishing returns.

All things are **tools** to be used for different purposes depending on where one is at. Your experiences of a spiritual high are no different. They point to something, but that something relies on your freewill; it doesn't exclude it. One sees what one wants to see, and that is based subconsciously on what speaks to you as your treasure. But when in doubt, try not to overlook that there is something far deeper that is always being pointed at, and the evolving soul knows this inherently, and you will as well, no matter what you focus your perception on today. That is the true gold you run away from when you seek solitary pleasures as a manner of replacement. Go to the gold today, ready to receive, ready to share, and the secondary solitary pleasures will fade from purpose. If you search your heart, you will see that this has always been your experience on this path. The heart of communion is union.

Soberly, a part of you may say today, *"There I go again,"* as you observe the drunk descent to pleasure for quenching or distracting your attention from suffering. In your practice, attempt to pay attention to this process today, and affirm the innocence at its root. You descend in this way to attempt to fulfill your only **one true desire**: to be One with God; to be your true self. As we've said, from this substitution you would be wise to not conclude that Oneness with God is equal to fireworks, thunder, and lightning, or that heaven-sent high we spoke of. Oneness with God is merely the one need to know oneself truly, without guile or pretense. To be relaxed within this state of awareness-of-awareness is as natural as you are. What is unnatural is to replace this for something far less. To love fully, including yourself, nothing can ever be powerfully alluring enough to divert your attention away. Hence God is your strength, and vision is His gift. You are living truth, and you need not chase effects or substitutes.

The **excitement** of awareness-of-awareness is much like the initial excitement of a lucid dream, where you recognize you are dreaming. That bright, excited, unstable state that often leads one to lose lucidity faster than they'd have wanted, or to wake up from the dream state altogether, is much like the excitement of the recognition that *you are truly alive.* With seemingly countless cycles, awareness-of-awareness turns ever so gently into self-abidance, or a stable state of lucid living grounded in a simple *recognition of self.*

Because of this, **everything can drop away** in your morning meditation today. Attempt not to lose focus on the sobriety of your mind. The main idea and the first stage of this practice period is very standard and simple enough: focus on sight as comes from the vision of I Am. The second phase is where you apply it to each object arising. In later cycles, you may accomplish this without any mind wandering. For now, if it does happen, gently pull it back.

Today we attempt a recognition beyond I Am merely informing our sight. True perception is only useful while you are perceiving, and all perception is **perceiving outside of God**. You perceive with ego. You can heal perception to receive or see by asking guidance from the Holy Spirit. He brings you to I Am, yet fully reunited in I Am you do not see, for perception is unnecessary. Our use of perception is thus replaced by knowing. In God you know because you are One. You do not need to see.

In your practice periods, first hold the thought, *"I cannot see apart from God."* In time, allow this to transition to, *"Yet, in God I cannot see."* When you transition from perception to knowledge, perception and this thought simply drops away. You can come up for air to hear that same thought once again; but then again, all can drop away.

When done properly, you will feel a stillness so peaceful and so comfortable, like what you could feel when absorbed in a channeled voice, a lecture, a podcast, or a piece of music. These are tantric practices of being present as a receiver. Today, simply attempt to be within the here and now, you as the here, you as the now. Experiencing this, you would say that no feeling of time or space existed. In dream yoga this is called **clear light** experience where it occurs consciously in deep sleep between lucid REM dream periods.

Early in the cycles your ego will want to jump in and say that this is an amazing experience. Yet, to be honest, the experience will simply be the quietest you've ever felt. You experience it every night **between dreams**, but you just don't recall it consciously. It appears like it's hiding out always underneath every attentive absorption of your mind. You know, you could spend all day there, focused, and not be hungry.

Yet you cannot get there through your efforts. In fact, there is no *delineated place* to go *to*. You can only work to be asymptotically close to experiencing your unitive being and then God takes **the final step** and pulls you into heaven, which is not a place, but your eternal nature.

By final step, we don't mean you're all ready to not reincarnate again. It simply means you wake completely, and time/space drops away, only to return once again. You may even experience the image of God grabbing you up today depending on your spiritual framework of belief, but this is not important. The final step today may be unexpected, yet all you will know is that the little you didn't do it. Only I Am can. This is how you will know it is real.

Day Nine
The Cord as Code

The cord naturally is pulling gently. For today, don't try. Don't pull away. Don't swim, thrash, or try to repeat yesterday's victories. They are not now. The cord holds the code, as does the boat and the skier. Excitement is not warranted here. Let go of trying to control the movement. Let go of the effort.

The Son could never leave God, except in his belief he has. Yet in his belief he has a great deal of freedom on this elastic cord to go almost anywhere on this lake of experience.

Imagine, if you will, a speedboat where you are water skiing, connected by an elastic cord. In this metaphor, the speedboat is the one Father, the cord is the Holy Spirit, and you are the Son. The Son could never leave God, except in his belief he has. Yet in his belief he has a great deal of freedom on this elastic cord to go almost anywhere on this lake of experience. Still, he's **always tethered** to the one Father, for without this no life, or movement of the skier on the lake could ever exist. The lifeforce originates from the animating boat, the prime mover.

Now, you steer or maneuver as a skier by sight. The **paradox** in this is as follows: you cannot see apart from God, whom you're never truly apart from, yet, in God, reunited with God the Father, you cannot see. The first means that if it were possible to do the impossible and cut the cord from the one Father, then you wouldn't exist, and sight would be impossible. The second means that once you're back in the boat, in the unitive state, there's no means or purpose for sight. It's only required so long as you are skiing.

In the boat, as **the trinity unified** in God, one cannot perceive the lake as well. In fact, the lake, as the world you see, arises in perception only due to your illusion of experiencing something outside of God's Oneness, as when an infant first opens their eyes. So, inside the boat you cannot see. And apart from God there is no sight because there is no being. Sight only exists while you seem to experience things outside of self, and outside of self *is* outside of God. Sight is possible only through the enlivening of your being through I Am, by God. As you experience life you may get closer to the boat and other times you might get further away. Through your practice you experience this as the increased vision of mountaintop effects, or decreased vision through trying so hard to replicate the same effects. Doing so drags you down.

God is the entire setup: the boat, the skier, the cord, in triune form. In union all are God, God is One, as much self, as Father, as cord/code. **World is animated** and arises from the act of skiing. If no skier, then no boat, no cord, and no lake need arise. All would be One in God, and there would be no need for sight. Perhaps a world which exists apart from seeing truly has been what you wanted to see? We ask, how would a planetary illusion appear to you? What makes one illusion any different than the next? Earth is merely one sphere in an infinite tapestry of life, and its aggregate beliefs are informed by the common set of experiences of all who are part of it and are local to it. Now, **no effort** is required to allow the cord to reel you in closer to union in God. The cord naturally *is pulling gently.* For today, don't try. Don't pull away. Don't swim, thrash, or try to repeat yesterday's victories. They are not now. The cord holds the code, as does the boat and the skier. Excitement is not warranted here. Allow now to be now: on this lake, in this moment. Let go. Not of the cord, for that is not possible, but let go of trying to control the movement. Let go of the effort. Allow God's Love through the Holy Spirit to reel you in.

Be sure, you will bounce around a bunch as you get used to these dynamics. This is OK and it is part of **life in flow**. Through your connection, as you trust I Am, or trust your vision of I Am, you will strengthen the effect the cord has to guide you. You will trust in the give-and-take, in the back-and-forth, in your very being. You will ease into a life guided by something other than ego. Don't be quick to judge your progress based on if you seem to come closer to the boat occasionally. That is a peak experience and can be for many reasons including first successes. Remind yourself lovingly; first successes are based on learned skills. Skills, like sight, are not needed where you are going. They are a temporary way to teach and learn. In the end, you will ski nearer to God without a single skill. It is your natural inheritance. It is what you are. You learned separation. Now you must gently unlearn it. In time there you will perceive no separation from the boat, and then sight itself will cease. Your brother will be seen as self.

The Holy Spirit has always existed with the Son while in union with the Father. Only in the Son's dream was the Holy Spirit purposed to be the cord, or your link to God and brother. Yet, He is eternally **the code**, our spiritual DNA. *"The cord is the code; I will to ask,"* is an excellent meditational mantra for today. Another way to express this is, *"God is the triune Source; I cannot see apart from Him."* As God is source to Son, so God is source to Father and Holy Spirit. Thus, this simple meditation is a **giving to God**. You choose to see the Holy Spirit not only as a connecting link in the dream, but as the *code eternal.* By *giving* to the Holy Spirit this charitable perception, you open yourself to *receive* instead of reliving prior successes or over-focusing on progress. This is giving with no expectations as informed by Love. *All* movements on this lake are infused with God's Love and joy of being, including the bouncing around. So today, take time to enjoy the successes *as well as what often appears as* **lack of success**. They are *all* for a purpose of learning to ski by letting your awareness of I Am guide you. Go to the Holy Spirit and ask for guidance. Literally ask out loud and listen to what arises.

Today, take time to close your eyes and practice **sinking down**, and further down into self. You're tethered, don't worry. Notice the thoughts which go by. They start from below and you pass by them as you descend similar to a deep-sea diver with a heavy weight. As you continue, they become fewer and slower in their pacing. Then stop noticing and let them go. The environment of your mind apparently becomes lighter, and you notice what you are in your core: Light. It's always there, but the clouds of thought block it, day in and day out. As you enter more the light, even the diver image falls away and you're floating in this abundance. You've traveled here *through* the cord to the home of your awareness. No matter where you dive, you thus find yourself back in the boat, **in union**. You hear the physical world when random sounds arise, or even the humming sound within your ears. In later cycles, you will find no need to resist whatever arises, or even grasp these items with thought. Let them arise. You may acknowledge them, but they no longer contain the truest you. It is now merely **a canvas** your essence manifests on.

You may notice that the concept underlying today's meditation seems opposite to yesterday's practice. Descending into the light testifies that I Am is the light in which you see. Yet, in perfect union with I Am, sight becomes meaningless. Meditating on either will bring you to a similar awareness of self, either focused on the illumination of things *by* I Am, or no need for illumination *in* I Am. You may notice one of these two meditations, **by God, or in God**, will bring you deeper and more honestly in union than the other.

Another idea is to consider, as a metaphor, the light around **the Sun** which your world lives and bathes in. I Am is that life giving light *within you*. Meditation on this will illuminate as you descend into self. As this happens, consider the inside of the Sun itself where no things can exist. No sight is possible there, merely merging. Meditation on the second idea will continue to focus on moving past the light of the Sun to the enveloping void, the no thing where all form cannot exist in union with the One.

Whatever method you choose today, go as deep as you like and **play** in the environment you find yourself. You are perfectly safe and always perfectly self. There is nothing else.

Day Ten
Extending Presence

We're all filtering the One Light differently, but we're One Light, not reflections of a light of God outside of us, but more a shared light that continues to bounce and irradiate everyone and everything. It animates us all. It animates everything by its very presence. It's easy, while lost in our view of the world, to take I Am for granted or look beyond it.

These identities are simply roles you each play. Each role is not all that you are. A role is a sort of dream you take on.

Today, you will begin to nurture the seed of a new meditational practice centered on **mind and heart searching**. Allow whatever bubbles up to present itself fully as you slowly repeat the phrase, *"I Am present within."* There doesn't need to be any sense of hurry. If discomfort arises, let go of the words for a short time and begin again, slowly. As these words are repeated, center first on God, I Am.

As objects arise, allow and acknowledge them, but remind yourself that this is an **image** that you have made. With I Am present within, you can as well choose to let it go by loving it fully, as it arises in I Am. There is no need to push away the thought or image or deny its presence. In much the way like an old loving grandmother you can learn to say to an image:

> *"Look sweetie, I am happy to spend time with you talking over coffee and tea, and you can stay as long as you like, but you and I both well know that that's simply not true. I can show you what's true by loving you. So please stay, I'll make you a bed if you choose to, and we can even talk in the morning."*

In this way, Love wraps its arms around the image and **helps it unfold** gracefully, enveloping it without fear. It is not trying to squeeze it to death. It is just allowing the dirty cloth to soak in the warm soapy water, without a need of scrubbing. The dirt slowly leaves as no more purpose is found in it.

This **self-reflection** is filled with acceptance and comes from a deeper recognition of the observer-self accepting imperfection without being affected or wounded by it. You're beginning to recognize that there's so much you missed in your ignorance of non-observation, habitually lowering yourself to be in need of defense, as a victim, as falsely vulnerable. Yet, you also give up your truth by quickly assuming the weakness, the smallness, the vulnerability which seems to fit, and reacting to it as if it were the ultimate truth of who you are. In doing so, you do not pause to ask what this choice you make is telling you.

This is an important step to cultivate a mindset of not being **misidentified** as the victim or even demanding personhood as a form of dominance or control, others being submissive to what you think you are. How do your own decisions reflect on the importance of this circumstance in your own life? What does your ego believe this circumstance is for? Are you choosing to side with this blindly because it feeds your separate needs in a zero-sum game? This is the game where if you don't take yours quickly, someone else will. Then there will be nothing left for you. Sound familiar?

You're opening to what initially appears as a new way of seeing, yet it's a seeing you've always had, where life is in fact not a **zero-sum game** at all. Take, for instance, an idea. Ideas which are shared strengthen, as they cannot leave the domain of consciousness. Extending as they do, they are not limited quantities. You may be able to see this in certain circumstances. But you are being called to generalize this learning to include *everything real*. The moment you recognize that you are an idea in the mind of I Am, something *will* shift. You extend. You are not limited. Personhood is limited, but you are not just a person.

One's inalienable individual rights are testimony to the growing heights of your incremental learning. Just as two-thousand years ago, these ideas would be foreign and dangerous, so too today our true nature calls us into what appears as the unknown. The idea that the individual is *the* divinely sanctioned quantum of God is not the apex of your learning but can be the **basis for grander ideas** of who you are. If you can make the leap now, you will make your learning so much more efficient. You are so much more than the personality. Consider this today.

Other additional examples: give a hug, a smile, or a compliment. These things strengthen the awareness of our bond of union. Happiness arises through a circular motion beyond where we as a person could ever touch. The constructive nature of I Am doesn't fight personhood. Never forget, **personhood** *clothes it.* I Am willingly assumes the form of personhood, perhaps to play, to dance. It's a dream character in some way. I Am in you enlivens. You will lay down your personhood one day when it is appropriate. And this process doesn't have to only be at physical death.

It's simply a **way of seeing**. That's all. You live. You are life. Awareness doesn't terminate. The type of world we see terminates or transforms when we die, just as it does when we awake from a dream. The type of world we see can change at any time, and this is your choice. At some point this week, pick a morning or two, and go into this idea as you awaken from a dream. The dream felt real. Now unless you're lucid, almost all the time you awake in the morning and take it for granted you had amnesia and willingly forgot the higher context of waking life to this singular dream. So too is spiritual awakening in waking life as lucidity is in your nighttime dreams. When in the ego you willingly forget the higher context of spiritual life to your experience in this world as a body.

It can be momentary: a surprising revelatory experience that you're I Am. We're all filtering the **One Light** differently, but we're One Light, not reflections of a light of God outside of us, but more a shared light that continues to bounce and irradiate everyone and everything. It animates us all. It animates everything by its very presence. It's easy, while lost in our view of the world, to take I Am for granted or look beyond it.

You can see the same as experienced in every role you play, whether it be father, mother, friend, coworker, husband, wife, son, or daughter. They are **roles**, and as such, each role is not all that you are. A role is a sort of dream you take on. It is a constructive dream in many cases, with a lot of truth flowing back and forth. A shared dream occurs when the roles assumed are embraced by both. You will see this as your children grow into adults. All are equal, as a member of the Sonship, each manifesting uniquely as a filtered version of God as the code. Investigate this as you share your presence with your loved ones. Be they older or younger, meet them where they are. See their divine potential, even when they appear meddling or selfish. You may have been with these souls in prior lives. Most relationships have gone through many cycles.

Not that this matters so much in this very moment except to contextualize that these identities are simply roles you each play. And the roles which may appear challenging, stressful, or even destructive can serve a higher purpose, by **your agreements** to take these specific roles on in your lives. Perhaps there is a karmic debt to repay in a constructive manner. To see how your choices affect others is invaluable and accelerates your dance in space and time. Consider it as one of God's appendages sending a signal to another appendage, *"Hey, that hurt when you bent me back like that!"*

Only in your **shared unlimited being**, which includes everything and everyone, can this be truly communicated. If you were truly separate, you would not have the potential for communication *at all*, as you'd be in a separate universe. The fact that you have this potential is testimony of your *One Life*, not only on this planet in the physical, but also in spirit.

Day Eleven
Pause for Feeling

Today, be gentle, and open yourself up to feel sensation as you visualize the light. The more you practice this visualization, the closer you get to living enlivened by God's light across all your energy centers.

Feel God's light shining in you as a joyful openness.
Let it arouse your spirit and body as you wish.

First thing today, close your eyes, and for this moment **feel God's light** shining in you as a joyful openness. Let it arouse your spirit and body as you wish but be certain to stay in the warmth. Visualize God's light pouring through all, not only you. Experience this as a grounding of your present feelings to the whole of creation.

Take slow deep breaths as you feel the energy rise within your body. Anywhere it balls up in you, use your breaths to dissipate it before it overcomes that specific **energy center**. Take note of the centers, or chakras, where the largest sensation is not present. Spend time with yourself and the divine within, spreading the energy and letting it flow. For instance, if you feel energy in your lower body but not in your head, visualize in your breathing the energy flowing from your sacral center or solar plexus towards your throat and head by passing through your heart. Your heart will open even more.

Today, be gentle, and open yourself up to feel sensation as you visualize the light. Do this throughout your day as often as possible. A deep joy of being in communion can be experienced at each application to reinvigorate you and help you feel sustained. Do you feel appreciation? Do you feel your own spirit extending? Do you feel it deeply throughout your body? Does your heart feel open? Be mindful of what today's practice reinforces in you. At some point, you may sense the purpose of tightening up to be quite unnecessary. If you do allow yourself to feel something akin to an orgasm, this is not a failure or a mistake, as it is the **lifeforce** expressing itself.

The more you practice this visualization, the closer you get to living enlivened by God's light across all your energy centers. The physical response is not the cause, but only the effect of it, as manifested through this spontaneous choice to feel. It cannot be planned or repeated to gain the effect. And **do not attach** to it, or it will all stop. Rather, open to *give yourself* to God. Love the life around you. A part of everything is here with you.

Day Twelve
Alignment of Thought

Whenever you're in alignment, you will find no game of hide-and-seek. The joy of the simple child's game captivates you still, though is often played in a fearful manner. In the mind of I Am there is no hiding or seeking. Attempt to see this in your thought-practice today.

Pretending to hide and seek after gaining awareness
is still fine, but we want to remind you that
alignment will give you the greatest joy.

All thought appears in the mind of I Am, for I Am *is* the mind with which you think. You remain in ignorance and hold back your mind from that which you know when you're living life informed by your own ideas of separation. Consider this carefully. There are **three modes** with very clear progression. The first mode is ignorance; the second, awareness; the third, alignment. While the move into awareness is an awakening from ignorance, it only testifies to a short-lived agreement. Alignment is a long-lived agreement. While in awareness, you may choose in an unaligned fashion, in play. You always have this choice in any of the three modes. Notice that you *do* play that way and you are not interested in giving it up so soon. This is fine, if this is what you want, but see it and call it for what it is today: a self-serving choice of the ego which enables a hollow activity of short-term pleasure seeking.

Whenever you're in alignment, you will find no game of **hide-and-seek**. The joy of the simple child's game captivates you still, though is often played in a fearful manner. In the mind of I Am there is no hiding or seeking. Attempt to see this in your thought-practice today. This is not a sinking down like in prior lessons. It is a rising up towards perfect innocence. Your mind in I Am is forever innocent, once you let go of your young thoughts of separation. Young, because you've not always played the game, but have just begun to recognize that you are. If you investigate within, you will see that your original nature tells you that this is so. Your prior practice of sinking down testified to there being so much more than frantic sight or splintered will. Therefore, you can be assured that today, while rising up, you'll find so much more than separate thought and the game of pretend.

You're holy and singular in the mind of I Am, and this mind is ever-present in you. Align for moments as you practice. Sense the tree as roots today. You are but one root branch and can help feed the whole organism. Choose thoughts **aligned with I Am** and God's tree will grow, the kingdom of God as seen in this world. Your mind aligned nourishes the whole world. Your mind separate maintains its ignorance. Yes, a big thought. Yes, perhaps a spiritual movement from playing adult to being one. Pretending to hide and seek after gaining awareness is still fine, but we want to remind you that alignment will give you the greatest joy. Delight in moments of it today.

It is a wake-up call, and you truly love **the innocent mind** it brings. The kindness overflows in you. The feeling of openness and lack of guarding a position dissipates quickly. There is no position to guard. There is nothing but joy of freedom like a small child once again. You're able to see as one, able to be as one, choosing to think as one from within. These are not thoughts married to complex application. These are unifying thoughts underlying all application. No matter what is chosen or acted upon by self or other, Life is One. The tree is whole. Love pours forth to be all that there is, from within.

The totality of this Love captivates the split mind. It makes subservient such a mind, by **pouring Love** over it, and the separate mind aligns without a second thought. That may be new for you. It's a more massive alignment of acceptance overlaid on everything in this moment. It's *agape love* in a more real form than you've yet experienced. It's full of appreciation.

Be excited to make this a day of this **new innocence**. Early in the cycles, you may overlay it on I Am as a separate state. There may seem to still be fearful play with an undo-mode standing in for joyousness, and sometimes it may truly feel like pretend, even when it isn't. Remind yourself that this self-trust is *a start* to enliven the child within you to be less fearful and more truly playful.

Day Thirteen
Shared Consciousness

As you practice today, you may be expecting more serious, fearful situations to come to mind. But what comes to you now is a re-realization about God's strength, a re-remembering which informs your power. Yes, you can instantly sink into the strength of I Am and completely diminish all traces of spiraling trails of thought, the very thing that used ruin your morning or your day.

All characters in your dream symbolize an aspect of you
in I Am; and time, although fluid, feels quite real.

Surprising as it is, you are dabbling in your dreams into the area of shared consciousness. Remember, all characters in your dream symbolize **an aspect of you** in I Am; and time, although fluid, feels quite real. You may see flashes of light as you sleep or go to a timeless, peaceful place of no objects occasionally. These are all meditative manifestations of the mind which has stopped its seeking behavior, seeing that when you seek you mostly only window shop.

The **power of your mind** is without compare; of that you know. So much can be recognized in such a little time, and this also is a testimony to shared consciousness, which can feel so polarizing an experience as a first date, a good shower, or a roller coaster ride. You will know it by the good feelings which accompany it. The recognition of truth is *always* accompanied by joy. This is how you know. Truth recognized is always joyous. And it is this to which you are being called.

In your everyday life, there is no relationship between what is real and **what you *think* is real**. Zero relationship in any respect. This means it's all up to you; literally! As you choose to see it all, *you are asking the Holy Spirit* to transform your sight. You can claim *all* of God's knowledge to be yours and open yourself up to receive. Yes, you have that power. In later cycles, you know you're already open to it. Simply sense it today, and it is so.

Yes, a big stupid smile overcomes you as you go deeper. Your pride dissipates and you are sustained by self in I Am. You are One. Feel your lightness of being as joined in One thought. In earlier cycles, you will need to be reminded of your **potential for insanity** more than anything else, as under all your senseless thoughts and crazy ideas which clutter your mind are the thoughts you thought with I Am in the beginning. What does this exactly mean? Notice how insane you get when you disconnect from Love and are under the influence of the ego. In later cycles, the highlighting of your innocence infusing your original thoughts will connect you to God's Oneness and all your loved ones. For now, reflect on this, and allow it to be your calling.

As you practice today, you may be expecting more serious, fearful situations to come to mind. But what comes to you now is a re-realization about God's strength, a re-**remembering** which informs your power. Yes, you can *instantly* sink into the strength of I Am and completely diminish all traces of spiraling trails of thought, the very thing that used ruin your morning or your day. This morning, envision it as levitating down beneath crazy, dense clouds, dipping into God's light, which triggers the light to shoot upwards, totally clearing the way. No spiraling thought-trails or emotional clouds to be found; gone, just like that.

Each time you go to this state today to re-clear, the idea of it being **a mental state** stops completely. For a while you'll see some thought-trails below or above the prior thought-trails. It is fine, because you know you'll find greater elucidation each time around this *beneficent spiral*. Each time around this spiral you elevate some, join the polarities, and converge to a clearer solution. In a vicious circle you go down a bit more and *diverge further*. Ego learning is like this, *always* incremental, up or down. Note that this may happen while getting distracted from your meditation today by a negative thought spiral when you have time to think. It can happen anywhere; really, any place where your mind tends to wander.

You can realize *this* is what the strength of I Am is truly for: to **clear** the mental state **and reset**. These situations may seem trivial, but being tempted so often by your thought-trails, or monkey-business, all of it tends to grow into a monstrous three-ring circus. The strength of I Am stops it in its tracks, no more spiral. You can *always* choose to sink down and in. Yes, this is shared consciousness in God.

In later cycles, it may feel redundant, as you've brought yourself to similar conclusions, yet somehow, it hits you harder every time. It isn't redundant, because you can then become more aware of other monkey-games you're trying to get away with. **Fear not**! Such is the domain of one finding their way once again. Reflect on this today. Whenever you're afraid, or think you've lost your way, God *as your neighbor* is right there with you. I Am in your brother is the same I Am in you. Let this come to mind as the monkeys attempt to carry you away. Let it remind you how easy it is to sink down and in.

As you experience each cycle, each elucidation of an everyday experience *shifts*, for you to see what's your core and what's the overlay. No one not experiencing this can ever grasp it. Yet, you do. At first, you start to sense that the overlay may be the infinite spiritual nature momentarily experienced. Over time the overlay becomes clearer, as the physical limits which seem often experienced yet are less and less constraining. No matter how, in time, the secondary truth becomes the overlay; and the first primary activity becomes the truth of what you've known yourself always as. This is *the remembering*. These are the very same **shared thoughts** you thought with I Am in the beginning.

Then the clouds never seem to cover the sky, or only occasionally. It may still happen from time to time but the sky becomes so deeply clear that you notice it was more an act of *unlearning the clouds as you*. When you only see a **patch of blue sky** you can be forgiven if you mistake it for the rare event or special state, and you interpret the clouds as seemingly ever-present you. But as the clouds go, you see what always remains. Even if the clouds cover over fast again in a few minutes, or hours, days, weeks, or months.

In later cycles, the special event becomes when the **clouds come back**, not when clouds go! Suddenly, you're surprised you got wrapped up in insanity for a change. For today, seek to make peace with time and think the thoughts you think with I Am. See how far you've come. See how the momentary loss of sight cannot obstruct the sky no more. Renew your resolve to find the way back to sharing One Consciousness, to unlearn all you've learned, and to be whole.

Day Fourteen
The Implication for the Universe

This universe is abundant with life, and each sun is an experiment in reunification. Sit with and rest in this acknowledgement today as you spend time in nature, feeling the Sun's rays, and the end of this, our second week.

The universe is not only teeming with life, but is the very manifestation of it, embodying spirit in all manner.

You are realizing more the implications of God's sons and daughters being **connected to One Source**. Many eyes, many perspectives, One I Am. Imagine a wheel with God's children gathered around, each with a conduit linking their mind to the energy source at the center of the wheel. You've borne witness to it throughout your life as the spark or connection in everyone. Some choose to shift and turn their heads in such a way that the conduit becomes misaligned and cannot serve its purpose. But all it takes is a gentle shift to realign the conduit to receive the energy of I Am and to access the thoughts of I Am.

You can see all God's children as your **neighbors** on this wheel. What appears near or far from the perspective of the rim is equidistant from the hub. Whoever appears as next to you on the wheel may seem to share your perspectives with slight differences, and you've most likely already found a common inner voice you both share, whether or not you give credence to it as your higher self. When aligned, you share the mind of I Am, together. This applies to someone seemingly across the wheel as well.

At the point you appreciate the one creation, you are ready to receive openly the conditions arising from our unity and become a citizen of the galaxy. It will be received with humility, or it will not be received at this time, because such a true citizenship must enliven you honestly. And all things you thought you saw truly will transform to their true nature. You each manifest the energy of I Am as a unique solution within life's grand cycle of incarnations you've chosen. This can be said at any level of gradation. At first, anything that would appear as a stark difference in perspective can be seen from a **singular framework** which approximates your union. There is a grain of truth in all frameworks, some more than others. No, no teaching or book is perfect, as all must flow through the conduits available. You are the conduit; doubt this to your own delay.

All thought systems have some attempt at a comprehensive framework for the life of the spirit. When you find one for you, you'll know it. You'll find the very keys to creation are not beyond your appreciation. It is the very fact that **you cannot leave the creation** which enables you to reflect it, and reflect on it, no matter what approximation of it seems presented to you, by you. Place what doesn't speak to you by the wayside. Nothing true is lost in I Am. We are all One.

There's reason to use the tree and root metaphors we have thus far. All of creation rolls up together, and what Darwin discovered about all earthly biological life sharing a single evolutionary tree, is true as well for spirit. The DNA is unified, but manifesting in a filtered, seemingly fragmented sort of manner on each of the levels of manifestation. This universe is abundant with life, and **each sun is an experiment** in reunification. Sit with and rest in this acknowledgement today as you spend time in nature, feeling the Sun's rays, at the end of this, our second week.

What you see in physical form *is* the manifestation of a much larger, grander tapestry of **lifeforce manifesting** on the planes or spheres of existence. Your learning, once it passes through the earnest desire to appreciate creation through a unified framework, will be connected to everything, everywhere. The ship of your life turns slowly as you set a new course with new prayerful intentions, to reconnect all the network of energetic roots you put out into the unified field.

These are all manifestations of appreciation of the one hub, God's one Son as all creation. This is what Jesus saw so clearly that he was willing to see **no value in defense** or the concept of suffering. He took an intense martyr's path to express it, because your ego values high orders of perceived difficulty, not that you all must do the same as him. Seeing into the hub is the unification of mind. You think with the unthreatenable mind of I Am unified. You see God in all because you see only one life all share. You may each experience your separate path, and seem to experience physical death alone, but you are all testifying to the unity of all life, of the One, in every step. Today let the spirit within guide you, to share in this unified framework. As you do, you go onward with mighty companions and with a new mindset. You will share in the fruits of being within the unified creation more and more. You are being invited.

For those who are more focused on the us/them identity structure in this world, this invitation may come manifested through a fundamentalist orientation with more cautious experience sets. For those who focus more on relationships and context, the exact structure of their group identity including religious affiliation doesn't matter as much, and so the manifestations of appreciating all life come with a different slant stressing **greater acceptance** of others and is infused by new experiences.

As a soul evolves it focuses its incarnations on different aspects of life on the material plane. The five levels incarnating souls engage their focus on are survival, structure, achievement, relationship, and context. In these stages you will choose to learn and learn to choose in the material realm, the physical plane. When you complete all seven stages you join your soul family, or entity, comprised of approximately one-thousand soul fragments.

The wheel metaphor may be simplistic, but one could better visualize the structure of the creation as fractal nested hubs of hexagonally packed **groups of seven** spheres. Each grouping of seven fragments, or *essences*, occupies one of the next seven positions to other groups of seven in the next layer. Next on up, that grouping of forty-nine holds again one location in the next group of seven forty-nines. The trinity gives rise to these seven divine energies, as groups of two energies on each of the three axes, with a seventh energy being at the center of all axes. These are the seven primary sons, or attributes, of I Am.

No diagram is equal to creation, but while you are focused on the material, a diagram can help provide a conceptual framework for useful unitive contextualization. You will revisit this again and again in your practice, for it calls to you all as part of your planet's journey into the next density. As a planet you are taking the steps necessary to evolve into a **social memory complex**. While the emergence of your internet challenges your societies to find new ways to function, this challenge, coupled with your new ability to communicate, access, and utilize massive amounts of information as a collective understanding, is exactly what accelerates this evolution. You're far from the first planet to make the jump. Minds are perceiving their joining on a variety of levels, many constructive, and you are past the turning point as a planet to delay any longer.

Fear not, for as it comes, it feels more like home to those who have worked to usher it in. Joining will not remain foreign, even if the effects of such challenges may concern you now. There is a **forgotten song** which you will find you sing naturally. Your being guided to engage in this meditative cycle is but a part, an aspect or stanza of such a song. Be assured, it's a song you sang all the time, yet like all the separated, you lost awareness of it by attaching to the things of matter, believing they matter most.

You dream naturally because this is a direct reflection of the **astral plane**, what you experience whenever the physical world is unattended to. On bodily death it is the same. To dream is to create or project symbolically. You're almost always doing it, whether attending to the physical or not. In later cycles, you'll break through into your recognition of your astral/symbolic experience. All astral experience is also here and now but clouded by what appears the agency of an outside world.

The physical plane, everything material here on earth, is a massive, **shared dream** you all commit to, and one which has stability because of the number of dreamers dreaming it together. The stability doesn't demand it comes from outside your subjectivity, as your science would conclude thus far. Only in the last one-hundred years have you found that observation changes what happens.

Matter exists *in* consciousness and is made *from* consciousness. In fact, matter *is* conscious at some reduced level, as is everything cast to material existence. Nothing in your universe is dead, even if you have temporarily mis-defined life only as that of the biological kind. The universe is not only **teeming with life**, but is the very manifestation of it, embodying spirit in all manner. From subatomic life, atomic life, mineral and chemical life, viruses, and all the gradations of biological life on up through human life and beyond where self-agency becomes our shared experience, in this, your density, and the next in ours. In yours, self-agency naturally mistakes itself as arising out of the physical body.

The body is your out-picturing which your filtered essence embodies. It is the evidence of your spirit. It demonstrates to you and to others who you believe you are and what you actively see the world is. Jesus saw all of this and thus saw no true sacrifice in choosing to demonstrate a path of Love-filled martyrdom to your planetary illusions of hate and division. By being such a martyr, his highest self opened the door to your recognition that **the body is not the self**.

As you experience consistently the power of the astral present in the material, soon it gives way to your recognition of the causal, which is the level of intentionality that informs all symbols. Your spirit manifests and operates on all three lower, concrete planes simultaneously while you attend to the physical experience: the **causal plane**, the astral plane, and the physical. These planes are filled with currents of intentional, symbolic, and material forms all interacting.

Yes, even the spirit of minerals has an intentional and symbolic canvas on which to express itself, just so much more constrained and not as rich in **degrees of freedom** toward diversity as a plant, an animal, or a human does. All that embodies as material has intentional and symbolic expression. All is spirit.

Today, reflect on your world being just one form of the **experiment of expression** on the material plane within your galaxy. We assure you; your Sun has carried on many experiments in this dance of reunification and will continue doing so. Of this, biological evolution on your planet is one beautiful portion of this very experiment. You can be quite sure you're not alone; neither in yourself, your civilization, or your world as planet, solar system, or galaxy.

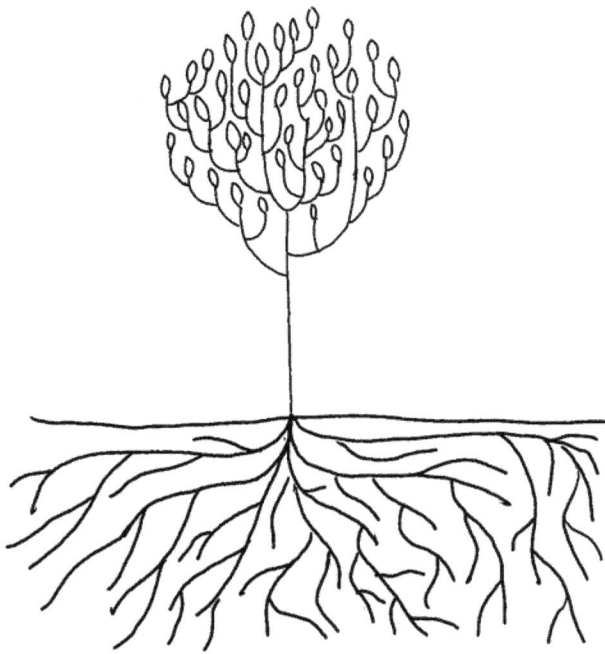

WEEK 3:

Transformation
& Consistency
of Practice

Day Fifteen
Forgiveness

In this moment, you either condemn yourself or forgive yourself. Today, you can see it as so. There is no other way forgiveness is called to you than by first nurturing an illusion about yourself. As you clear up your misthought about yourself, you forgive.

You hold the key to your own release.

God does not forgive, because He **does not condemn**, but His Love, the love within I Am, is the basis of all forgiveness you are called to find, just as ego fear is the basis of all condemnation. Whenever you've asked God for forgiveness, it was really asking it to a projection of God as personality, or in other words, the biggest ego you could imagine. It was an innocent misunderstanding. People want to forgive themselves, and they believe they can't, at least not until the big authority says they can, because He does. Also, it could serve an ego purpose to blame God for bad feelings, or even be a justification for holding onto anger and judgment, both judgment against self and other; there is no difference.

When you forgive, you **release yourself from illusions**. When you condemn, you bind yourself to illusions. In later cycles, you may recognize that you had a lot of forgiveness to do when you first started this process. You had grudges everywhere, mostly buried, but perhaps held in place by your fearful use of a sort of rational arrogance. Those expressions may have a smug, kind veneer if you love to play the angel whenever it's profitable. No matter: you are here now.

It can get quite chaotic as you liberate old, buried condemnation based on illusions and they are making their presence known for the first time in a while. The pain you still feel in some relationships testifies to **the grudge** underlying it. You can't yet tell why, but such a pain compulsively drives you to be closer to that person when near to their gravity. It's a negatively fueled feedback loop, leading to a matter-antimatter reaction to undo your own illusions. While you often live with it at a manageable level, you know you haven't fully let it go. That's telling you there's a part in you that you must forgive still, as it is merely being expressed as pointed at another, a child of God. And this testifies to your illusion.

In this moment, you either condemn yourself or forgive yourself. Today, you can see it as so. There is no other person which requires your forgiveness. In Oneness, or *I and I*, you would not ever need to seek forgiveness, and even here in duality you do not, as condemnation is a process of projection. There is no other way forgiveness is called to you than by first nurturing an **illusion about yourself**. As you clear up your misthought about yourself, you forgive.

No apology or recompense is needed. The Love that comes forth will do everything of its own nature. Of course, if others request or require an apology, so be it; you will be ready and willing to do that without an ounce of cost or resentment. You simply apologize for your mistake. And a mistake it was, so it's easy to do. You were in illusion to make such a silly mistake about the Son of God. It may not be helpful to tell them about it being a mistake of your perception, or the idea that you must only forgive yourself of your own self-condemnation. You may though, if it seems helpful. Some are presently ready to receive what their spirit craves, for as long as their perception isn't obstructed strongly by personhood. But never delude yourself that *God needs you* to apologize, or that *God in you* needs to *be forgiven* by the other. There is *nothing but illusion in those statements*. Only those who equate themselves with an ego believe they require an apology, and only those in God, as I Am, can give an apology freely, without cost.

While in illusion you believe the other holds the key to your goodness door. And once they unlock it by accepting your apology you can then feel better cause there is no one who condemns you. The truth is that *you* hold this image of condemnation in place *yourself*. And **you hold the key** to unlock that door and let it go as well. *You* choose to be *condemned* in your own view of the world's view of you, and your seriousness shows it.

Even if someone said to you, *"I can never forgive you for what you did to me!"* you still must believe in that image about yourself before you condemn yourself. There is no other version of forgiveness for the student of salvation, for any other version **demands payment for costs** unreal. In unified spirit, you gain and lose nothing except by your own hand.

Through this, *all of salvation* lies. Yes, all. Let go! **Laugh or cry** as release, as nothing of condemnation is worth holding onto. It is behind *every* crazy thought you have; we promise you this. It is your answer to setting up structures to manage the insanity. In forgiveness, the insanity goes, and no managing structures are needed once the self-condemnation leaves. Any grudge, any insanity, any illusion, any compulsion, any fear, any boastful thought, any comparison; all of it is held in place by condemnation. Consider the prayer:

> *"Father, forgive them for they know not what they do."*

It was the perfect prayer two-thousand years ago for bringing into your world. Humans were becoming ready to sense this. Nowadays humans are beginning to sense the following:

> *"I forgive myself all my illusions, for I was mistaken in the Son of God. I knew not what I did. Not truly. If I did, I could have never sinned. I could have never separated that brother from me in my own heart."*

This is for you. It is a cleansing. Let go! Express your sorrow for your own blindness, and in Love, accept yourself as mistaken. Love yourself completely.

All self-debasement, all greed, and all pleasure seeking as a substitute for God's Love is held in place by **condemnation**. All of these and more are your obstacles; and we will focus on these in week four. Yes, this is a theme you will revisit each cycle. You will know you are doing the work as you feel the weight off your own shoulders. Ignorance of your obstacles is heavy. True acceptance is light. In later cycles, you will feel light as a feather.

Forgiveness is simply the letting go of illusions which you find so **gratifying to your ego** to hold. Look deeper and you'll find they are not satisfying. There's a difference. The first builds up something false. The second releases you to your true nature. The building up gratifies you while you believe you are your ego. The ego is an activity only. The satisfaction comes because deep inside you know who you truly are, and no ego activity can deceive you forever or fully.

Today, search your mind and use **others as a means** for self-forgiveness. Anyone you do not like is a suitable subject, for there, separation is in your heart, and be sure that it is held in place by your own projected condemnation. This will put yourself in the position to forgive *yourself*. True forgiveness comes initially by application to what appears externally. It heals you internally by acceptance of your original nature, for yourself. This is the same original nature of all. It has been called by many as Buddha nature, or the Christ.

What are your blocks to forgiveness? A sense of unfairness? Being undeserving? Expecting vengeance or punishment? Look deeper to those items. What do they say about you as the Son of God? Perhaps that he believes he is worthy of separation, exclusion, special treatment, and even condemnation. None of this is true and deep down *you know it*. The *only* **proper response** to a brother is *appreciation* for the opportunity he presents you to join further.

You see your brother holding the dagger, preventing your joining. No. He holds no dagger. He extends his hand and gives you lilies by **opening to you** all his own distortions. If there's a dagger here, look towards your own hand. See the blood stain of what you would have done to him, and let it go. Release this burden. It hurts you more than you know.

Forgiveness doesn't mean always saying yes to activities with this person, to give into their wants over yours, or even to like them. There are no external obligations to fulfill. This is no forced acceptance. Forgiveness simply **lays down the debt** which you demand payment of, and of which you hide from yourself. Yes, you demand. Yes, don't kid yourself, you wish to play judge, draw blood, have revenge, for yourself or for another. You wish to be the one to balance the ledger. But under whatever righteous fight this destructive desire hides itself under, whatever clothes it wears, you must feel it is poison to your soul. This poison is yours and not of the other person.

So, for today, let this person give you the opportunity to see through their own ways. Let this person serve the Holy Spirit's function in I Am to point the way towards your own distortions. Let them guide you towards Love through your stuck energies. That is **your decision**. Bring them *nearer* to your heart. You need not even speak with them if the situation makes it imprudent or impractical. Take, for instance, the terrifying example of one's child being abused. Depending on the nature of the situation it likely would be impossible or even be imprudent to meet the abuser. Yet, forgiveness is what you are calling to yourself, even if you claim not to hear it.

There is no coercion in Christ. There is no mistaken identity. There is only union. Father, forgive them for they know not what they do; you know this was said two-thousand years ago. We ask you to simply *try* it today. You might just be ready. Forgive yourself for your mistake in placing yourself on God's throne of judgment and **mistaking your brother** for a killer. Let not your heart make your decision forever. Today, let your awareness of God-in-self, as I Am, teach you where your heart is wrong about God, about the other, and mostly, about the self. You are infinite in Love. It takes but an instant to let it go.

In later cycles, you may recognize that the **effects of your own poison** may seem to strengthen as you become more aware of your calling. There's a good reason for this, and it lies in the spiritual law of cause and effect as manifesting through the ego. But be not afraid. It cannot consume you. In the end, you hold the key to your own release. Experience the pain of that poison for as long as it serves purpose of your higher self. The pain may be quite acute but be assured it guides you to constructive use. It fulfills the best in you at any moment. And once the purposes of the shadow elements lose their constructive nature, you will let them go, and you will center in truth. You will move from a belief in constructive ego-cost to *no cost in Love.*

Don't run from the shadow, the poison, the pain. Confront it. Walk through it if you must, or better yet, invite it in, but follow it not down its illusory road. It's here, within, like your brother without, to show you the way to your buried light. Just by its presence. In fact, energetically, they are one and the same. Manifestations of the same energy within and without. The **fracture of your world** *is* the fracture of your inner world. The fragmentation of one must reflect that of the other. Unify what lies within under a new purpose, and what seems to lie without will hold a new vision. Both will intertwine in the light of I Am and bring you to a place where inner peace is more easily manifested. This is your inheritance.

Whenever you choose to claim it is up to you. But claim it you must, for you must be a son or daughter of God. Do not try to break out of the ego resistance through fight. The resistance drops away of its own accord once you see no purpose in it. It will come when you're fully willing. It may not be now, but do not deceive yourself that you need do anything to prepare yourself to receive it. **Love will wait** for Love to see. It is as certain as I Am.

Day Sixteen
Self-Acceptance and Self-Care

Check your own heart and make peace with it. Let it be as it is. We don't want you to feel pressured to be something you aren't in this moment. In this lies all of what you could extend to all others in your life. Be as you are.

Reconnect today with your playful child or teen inside.
What was their joy?

Today, don't rush. Rather, **enjoy where you are**. Everything, including each of your grudges, holds purpose here since you've made your decision to follow God, by simply attending to I Am. An equal measure self-care and a kick-in-the-pants; it cannot go wrong. For the latter, remind yourself what your feelings are telling you. Wherever there is turmoil, there is a lack of forgiveness. You may find yourself focusing on your **large offenses** but try to look around them for the evidence. If you make yourself blind to the depth of the main explosions, you will still see evidence of the fallout elsewhere. Using this evidence, through witnessing the effect on other relationships in your life, will help you stay sober and clear.

Let us assure you; you *will* move on from this point in a manner you think is *incomplete*. You don't yet see that an aspect of your seeing is now wholly true. You will have many more chances to right the ship. For now, it feels heavy and **hard to balance**. For today it is the best you can do. Accept and forgive yourself for that. This is an example of what lies next to the main grudges. Here lies some fallout. Here is where you can work with greater efficacy to see that all things work for the good. Here you can substantiate the lesson that I Am is the Love which informs your forgiveness. Check your own heart and make peace with it. Let it be as it is. We don't want you to feel pressured to be something you aren't in this moment. In this lies all of what you could extend to all others in your life. Be as you are.

Love for others is simply an application of self-love. Today, treat yourself as someone you are **entrusted to care for**. Speak to yourself with such goodness and welcome who you are. Be sure to include yourself directly as a benefactor of blessings. Even in direct application towards the outside world, you will naturally be uplifted by uplifting all in your sight. What blesses the world blesses you. What blesses you blesses the world.

You are a vital part of the Sonship. You are no different than anyone else. Bless yourself by seeing yourself as recipient of your own blessing. Nothing must be lost to be gained. No tradeoffs and no sacrifice. It's a day to **bless the world**. Your holiness does this, freely expressed. It is the most amazing shot of Love, and so easy to apply: just get out of your own way and laugh. Joy is the only whole state. Today is always a day to be joyous.

If applying during a dark moment, feel the sudden mood shift you're capable of by centering on being one who blesses, and one who is thus blessed. You uplift. You affirm. You create. You love simply by calling on the abundance within you. Sure, the **serious parts** of life may feel quite different than the playfulness, but if you can unlearn the seriousness just long enough to be earnestly playful in more things, then your holiness blesses the world. Sharing this with another is shared joy. Sometimes we're most gratified when we're called out by another, and sometimes we're gratified when we aren't. But either way, it's playtime that satisfies and which reflects the essence of our nature.

Reconnect today with your playful child or teen inside. What was their joy? Enliven this within you, not only by reflecting on the past but by staking the claim to today in this same energy. Allow yourself to be impish or impatient if you're usually in control. Whatever energy is freeing, let it flow. Dabble in it. Delve in. It's playtime. Self-love is filled with play. Give your inner child some good loving. Your child can then guide the way into a more joyful way of life with laughter and a light heart.

A loved child is a **naturally constructive** one. Let it lead the way.

Day Seventeen
Seeing into Perception

Once thoughts are slowed down easily you sense the visuals arise. Let them, but don't chase them. Don't believe in the dream today. Let the visuals arise with Love. Yet don't attach. That is the first step with perception.

When unmindful, your perceptions may carry you away into daydreams or fantasies and at nighttime into the world of symbolic dreams. Thought-trails may carry you away to monkey-mind.

Your ability to look into your heart and find a phrase, any phrase, which speaks of Love is *always* possible. Some examples could be, *"I Am Love,"* or, *"I Am wants the best for me,"* or, *"I hear I Am's voice all through the day."* Hold a phrase like this in meditation today, repeating it with your inner voice with your eyes closed. Each time, **slow it down** a little more and **allow space** to exist between the words of this phrase. As you continue to experience the spaces between the words, notice there is no need to think *outside* of the phrase. Your awareness of time slows down, and you open more space to witness to the eternal self, unclouded by objects. At some point the mantra itself *stops* in thought.

The visuals you may receive after your mantra falls away are objects of perception: dream like stabs at what your mind projects into reality to paint it as *you* wish. If you *pay attention*, you'll see that you experience this same phenomenon of perceptual images in sleep soon after closing your eyes, called hypnagogic hallucinations. While much insight can come from recalling your dreams, do not mistake these types of images for your goal today, which is to **experience lucidity**, a clear fullness of mind, as they rise and fall.

For you, thoughts are mainly in forms of words, and perceptions are in **the form of visuals**. When unmindful, your perceptions may carry you away into daydreams or fantasies and at nighttime into the world of symbolic dreams. Thought-trails may carry you away to monkey-mind. Neither object speaks directly of your nature, and so only captivates you when unmindful.

You don't need to follow the images, nor the thoughts, to be yourself. For instance, we in the astral don't communicate in words, as they are symbols of imprecise meaning. You can see this by observing that what a word means to one person isn't always the same to another. Notice in your meditation, your perceptions last *beyond* your thoughts, between them, and arise when your thoughts give room for them. In a similar way, we communicate in forms of thought-images like your perceptual ability, yet they do not **captivate us or carry us away** like your perceptions do to you.

To appreciate this, try once again your mantra and slow it down to the point where images arise. When you perceive a first visual, stay mindful and recognize that *it is an object diverting your attention* from the unitive state. You can then choose to follow the visual or remain sober of mind to hear my voice. My voice lies most consistently when you can focus, and this is most often experienced in inner stillness. Yet, in later cycles, you will notice that in your waking state, no perceptual visuals arise as you *tune in to me*. This is because you are engaged in the focused activity of ***listening and receiving***. And perception is different; when not listening or receiving, perception *pulls you into dreams*.

In dedicated meditation when you close your eyes you open your **mind's eye** to generate visuals more readily. Once thoughts are slowed down easily you sense the visuals arise. Let them, but don't chase them. Don't believe in the dream today. This sobriety of mind towards these hallucinations is, as well, a lucid dream initiation technique. It would be right to say that while you meditate, my voice is heard best when you're lucid. Lucid means conscious, not lost in perception. Let the visuals arise with Love. Yet don't attach. That is the first step with perception.

Try again, even on your very first cycle. As your mantra slows down, hear my voice. Let it speak to you. Visuals may still arise but notice they don't as much captivate you. **Focus on my voice.** Receive me, like a radio would a station. You will see it is not so deep by default, like a dream or a mystical trance. It can start on the surface by hearing my voice, your higher self. I Am ever present and as timeless as you are.

Now, you don't need to be actively conversing to be free of perception. I Am in the space between the words just the same. But for now, you may find it easiest to **have a conversation** with me within you. Notice, the restful state you experience between dreams, where there is no thought, no visuals, yet no conversation either. See? You're a pro! It is true you're not lucid in those moments, at least not often. Yet occasionally you are, and you simply don't recall them, we assure you.

Later today, see if you can **find time** to go to that place while staying in meditation. If visuals arise, see if you hear my comments on them. Focus on the comments, as slow as they may come, not the visuals. Sure, watch the visuals, but do not engage. You may nurture them, but do not attach. Keep it from moving into a dream.

We know you can. And you have.

Day Eighteen
The Blessed Distraction

Mystical experiences lie within the realm of spirit as manifesting through your causal, astral and physical bodies. As is the case, all such mystical experiences can be a diversion from the path when you overvalue them as an end in and of themselves. Enjoy them, they are flights of fancy, but note if you make them your gold.

Any meditative experience or state can produce startling sensations and visuals, whether it be in dream or in what you see as the waking state.

As we've mentioned, any meditative experience or state can produce **startling sensations** and visuals, whether it be in dream or in what you see as the waking state. This can include wonderful ecstatic physical manifestations of your higher emotional and intellectual centers impinging on your physical center, enlivening it energetically. Sometimes it's even hard to tell if it is more emotional or intellectual, since the experience is so extraordinary. As it begins, you may be letting go of heavy emotions and thus using deep quiet thought. Other times, you may be letting go of heavy thought and accessing deep secure emotional waves.

When you're enlivened in such a way, you're accessing **channels of energy** through your astral energy body that you haven't otherwise accessed routinely across a broad set of chakras. Sexual experiences could be similar, but more expressed through accessing the physical energy directly. Someone who is polarized in youth, perhaps by seeing other people's ecstatic religious experiences, will receive these experiences rather uniquely.

You would love to be able to believe in them and at the same time you may even be jealous of them. Someone who is physically centered can get deeply enthralled in sensations, including feeling the rain on one's skin, sweating, acts of physical affection, or even eating or drinking a tasty item. For them, meditation may be a rich **physical activity**. Think of the heaviness of the body compared to the ethereal. When physically centered and emotionally overloaded, you could be stuck wallowing in bad times and eating yourself from within your body, or elevated in good times using this connection to fly into the realms of the angelic bodies of higher frequency. The physically centered can access their physicality quickly if they shift that energetic mass into a higher domain. Those with a spiritualist attitude achieve this also, but differently, by belief.

You may have **ecstatic experiences** but access them through releasing thoughts, perhaps by channeling a voice and letting go of everything but that beingness which gives rise to such a channel. And all the way you may find yourself wrestling with your own skepticism and learning how to make a game out of letting it go and watching it return in various forms. As the chakras are filled with energy, your shoulders may feel as wide as the room, your head as wide as an ocean of expanse. It all depends on how you experience the energy flow through your throat chakra from your heart chakra up to your third eye.

Mystical experiences lie within the realm of spirit as manifesting through your causal, astral and physical bodies. As is the case, all such mystical experiences can be a **diversion from the path** when you overvalue them as an end in and of themselves. Enjoy them, they are flights of fancy, but note if you make them your gold. They are, in truth, merely the scent of the treasure, and not the treasure itself. You may feel on the cusp of something big. But the *content* of the experience isn't about gaining the deepest ecstatic, mystical, or supernatural trip you've ever had. It exists in simply recognizing your true nature which is Love.

You may feel at home in that state. If so, share your joy of being so open to this energetic experience. Nurture this part of you explicitly. And remind yourself often that it's *the Love that you are* which you are being permeated by, not by an *outside God* or possessed by some spirit. This is *your* lifeforce. This is *you unwrapped*. And so, if disturbance arises today and jolts you into being denser in the physical body simply go into the truth of the Love that you are always. No time, no ecstasy is required for that recognition. You can recognize I Am in *any* activity, including mundane ones. The activity of a spiritual orgasm is merely a unique one. As you grow, diversification and generalization of this experience will occur naturally. While intense visual manifestations during meditation are ways to experience the means, the end itself is always recognition of the true self, which can be **accessed directly**. We say all this because of the large temptation in the longer-term future for such a state to be over-valued by even the most disciplined. So, we warn you about these manifestations being an absorbing temptation. Do not overly focus on achieving them while practicing. If one does follow it as the treasure, it can become a distraction, a temptation, as all things can. See that Oneness *always is*. This includes the ecstatic forms of it. Therein lies the middle path to self.

Today, spread your holiness to everyone *within* you. Penetrate your own ideas about them. Feel the blooming of a world filled with such a celebration of life. You're **an ambassador** of it, and you're teaching it now. You've begun, and you will not lose this even if you put it down at some point; there's no going back. You've seen Love for what it is. It is you. You've seen acts of Love for what they are: a decision to see and act out of this new sight, to spread Love in our minds for all, to radically love and accept the truth of I Am in everyone, to see them penetrated by Love, as Love, constantly. The more you can witness in your mind to this open sharing the more it exists, we assure you. We promise you this: you do this and *the world changes*. All come towards the one celebration. Your influence is much larger than you know. Go help others see it by listening to them where they are at and sharing your Love with your own light heart. That radical Love as acceptance will penetrate everyone. You're not placed simply into a role of passivity or receiving here. You're able to *extend* Love into the world by *enveloping* ideas in your own mind. Ride that energy. Direct it. Drive it. Live it. Be it. The whole world joins you.

In later cycles, work towards **applying the attributes** to what you see as your nature in I Am. For instance, *"I Am Love. I Am full. I Am powerful, courageous, willing, beneficent, giving, and helpful."* There's a benefit to using singular words when you can. The primary focus won't then be on *what you can do* as much as it will be on *who you are,* which is your *inheritance.* What you can do in any instant relies on many things, but most importantly it relies on who you are. Describe to yourself the nature of that awareness. You are ever-present, eternal, unchanging, full, alive, open, willing to assume any form, and full of potential.

What may come to your mind are fearful attributes of what behaviors you believe you do not presently demonstrate with ease. For instance, the words *tireless* and *enthused* may strangely ignite your self-judgment. If so, take note that when not enthused about your tasks you may experience fatigue easily today. Part of you may just want to push the annoyance away by overlaying a pleasurable experience. Instead say:

> *"I know I Am not fatigue. I Am enlivened spirit. Even if my body or mind needs to rest, I can rest feeling connected to the enlivening power of spirit to rejuvenate my limited faculties on this physical plane. I can be sober of mind. I choose to be. I Am blessed as a son of God."*

Everyone who witnesses to separation has temptations to be **less sober of mind**. You run to these things to reduce your discomforts with some aspects of life. You are not your limitations, though your body and mind have them. You are more than your body and mind. Soon, you will return to the first day of the next cycle with this new recognition.

A useful counter-practice of the intellect for those caught in distraction could be described as the recognition of I Am within yourself through occasional **voluntary sensory deprivation**, and it is incredibly powerful. And relief of surface chatter would be immediate for when you attempt it. As you've experienced, your mind can tap into random noise when you're unfocused. In a sense, your mind is seeking to find a station broadcasting a signal. From this experience you can intuit that your brain is not the creator of consciousness, but rather a receiver of it, like a radio, which enables it to express itself in perceptive and physical reality. This informs a great deal of the psychedelic imagery when on hallucinogens.

The **three types of thought expression** are instinct, intellect, and intuition. Instinct is the basest, most animalistic, and reactive to the sensory experience. To a tired intellect, it feels very fresh and full of sensory truth, and things like breath, exercise, eating, and pleasure all testify to it. Presently in your society, intellect drives most thought-forms, and many mistake it as the apex of thought. Intuition is unified to the inspiration of the higher self, less reactive and rigorous, and more centered in the self which we're guiding you to experience.

When you practice disconnecting the intellect, initially your brain may get so habituated in focusing on the non-directed **internal chatter** of the monkey-mind. Mindfulness, which requires focusing on a singular, often sensory object of thought, can help reduce the symptoms like an aspirin for pain, but does little to find a cure. Through your practice, you become more aware of distraction and distortion, which increases pain initially. Mental awareness of internal thought-noise can become intolerable when it isn't stopped consciously. The truth is that you always have the power to center and stop freewheeling mentally.

You may recall a feeling of no thought in sex where you are lost in a parade of intense sensory rhythm. Imagine during your internal practice that you're clearing your mind and gently letting yourself sink into that same place of peace that sex gives, only you're not relying on the external rhythmic stimulus. We wouldn't be surprised if you orgasm doing it. Just don't judge your progress by those external manifestations. Sensing the **inner orgasm** may be a good way for someone so used to releasing their own ego in sex to reconnect to this internal state. Be careful to note that egoic sex imagery or fantasy is *not* the same.

You may have heard some refer to the instinctual way of finding I Am within as *tantric* and the less instinctual way as *yogic*. It's a duality which is made from the manner of seeking and that's fine. Tantric is more tribal, ritualistic, sensory, loud, plowing over thought. Yogic is more controlled, still, restrained, focused, dropping sensory experience away. Thus, the tantric method lends itself well to sexual practice. Tantric can be seen as letting go of false self *in* experience and yogic as finding self *within* controlled form, although this is a very large over-simplification. One is not more elevated or better than the other, though the yogic is inevitably more secure as it only relies on observing I Am in your stillness. This is the reason why many practices err on the side of conservativism and caution you to not engage in tantric practices. Today, especially in later cycles, try to recognize that *everything you do* has an amount yogic versus an amount tantric energy, and thus lies on a spectrum. Fear of the tantric may be a common mistake, but one you can learn from.

Tantric practices also include the **rhythmic auditory driving** experienced by listening to good music, dancing, laughing, or even experiencing tribal drumming. When searching your own nature in an unfocused manner, or lost in some internal noisy chatter, notice that this dissipates immediately with rhythmic music, or auditory driving, where you employ rhythmic sounds, such as drumbeats, to encourage brain cells to fire to the rhythm. This is done often to elicit unusual experiences in tribal cultures, but you can even notice it when it is non-rhythmic; the direct auditory stimulation reduces your own random mental chatter.

Try not to rely on getting lost in deep **fantasy or daydream** today, for now you see clearer into the distraction and diversions. Witness to the inner center which you can experience cleanly if you so choose. You may sense it and still in your stress choose to not turn towards it for years. If this is so, this is appropriate for how you choose to learn. Still, you'll see in such moments that you're habitually prone to stress, and you can learn to choose anew once you're willing.

Day Nineteen
God with You

You may miss the lack of responsibility which non-sober thought brings. Yet, it's all just a clever covering for the perception of life's hardness you experience. Under that perceived hardness is true life. The idea that I Am is with you always, no matter where you go, has the power to end all this foolishness forever.

Affirming that I Am goes with you is the way to curing any sense of loneliness and abandonment.

Do not beat yourself up over going to the old stress releases. When **old releases resurface**, all you *must* do is laugh deeply from within your center. We have long been very loving and accepting of you following any desire which arises for your own mental health. Until you sense the delay, you will delay even if you abstain. So please use the old release with a cheerful heart, but know it delays you without you seeing it. When it feels right, float in the question of, *"Does it hold a key?"* or, *"Where does this door lead?"* It doesn't necessarily have to be a bad place. Sometimes your old releases are the easiest way to get to a local mental health goal. This is not the long-term goal, but incarnated souls rarely play the long-term game 24/7. If you did, you wouldn't be here in the first place. Yes, being born is even a delay. So, accept and enjoy it for what it is. The dark can be a friend in what it shows you. Whatever arises, use it.

Regardless of the **many substitutes** you may have invented for what you believe to be the ills of the world, or others, the one thing you have not done is question the reality of the problem you sense. Its effects cannot be cured because the problem is not real. The idea that I Am is with you always, no matter where you go, has the power to end this foolishness forever. And foolishness it is, regardless of the serious forms it may take. This becomes self-evident after many years of practicing.

You may miss the lack of responsibility which non-sober thought brings. For example, basking in the childish pleasure of getting lost in the intoxication of some ideas, like a shared fantasy or reveling in special relationship feelings. Yet, it's all just a **clever covering** for the perception of life's hardness you experience. Under that perceived hardness is true life. You still need to remind yourself of that when tempted. Let the hardness idea truly go. You don't need the multilayered solution you've sought to solve that trouble. Instead, repeat, *"I Am is with me."* All fears and their effects drop away, and the heaviness of submission or expectation fades.

You also would benefit from remembering two things. First, **the why** is not important when talking about changing the effect of illusion to choose truth. Second, it costs nothing to choose truth. Do not give into non-joyousness. You can do it. Simply reset the switch and love! At first, you just have to smile. Yes, smile at life. Honestly, a day like today is filled with the simple pleasures of just being. It can amuse and uplift you. Look on it with honest joy of the absurdity. It will be hard for you to even write or read these words without a stupid smile coming over you.

Affirming that I Am goes with you is the way to curing any sense of **loneliness and abandonment**. Yes, those are big words, so in the earlier cycles you may not yet be able to see this. Ask yourself if loneliness and abandonment take shape for you in your shadow work or known fearful responses to life? If you answer no, the fact still remains: the practice of your laughter *will* relieve any sense of loneliness or abandonment. At this point, we know you better than you do. As surprising, insulting or as offensive as this may be, it is a true statement. It may just not be an area you often focus.

You may not claim that your aloneness is lonely or is informed by a sense of abandonment anymore. Yet if you look back you may see that as a child you felt abandoned at some point. You like to claim that you're over it, which may genuinely feel true, yet there must be more to it because of the very observation that a practice of laughter **unleashes your joy within**; in this way, I Am goes with you. If joy comes when doing this, it must indicate that a sense of loneliness or separation goes with you. Your joylessness, when it arises, shows you believe you are separate.

You may presently find great joy in alone time and yet not ever really feel blunt loneliness. Or maybe you just **don't yet see it**. This loneliness can take many forms, not just the simple crass kind of mourning circumstances of life on this physical plane, which may seem like a blunt emotional hammer to you while you see others complaining of it. Maybe it comes as an overall feeling of distance from life's dynamics, for instance. You may also find some of your relationships or hobbies attempt to replace that longing with other things. Maybe the loneliness manifests as a disturbance from the sense of being misunderstood by others, informed by a desire to simply feel like you are seen and accepted or understood as you are. We will explore these things in finer detail next week. For now, simply open to the potential that the experience of starving for affection or connection from parts of your youth is also presenting the same distortions, perhaps in a clearer form. In the end, if it is a sense of separation you want to believe in, then it will be there for you to feel, young or old. Acknowledging it helps you get closer to letting it go, through inviting it in fully and loving it with God's Love. Spend some time today looking into your youth for examples.

Regarding attraction, the **attraction of bodies** is a work of the ego and only attests to a limited and false view of who is worthy of your acts of Love and attention, often based on a physical beauty. It separates more than joins, and it testifies to hate more than it testifies to Love. Hence why performing a sexual act itself cannot ever be the cure for a sense of separation. Using anything in God's creation as replacement therapy devalues it, even if you don't see it at first. Most in your society have had experiences of their own love metered out in some ways based on special attraction, physical or otherwise. The less it is, the happier and more connected you will find yourself to be during that hour or day or week. By doing so, we extend Love from Godself to Godself, or from *I Am to I Am*.

Without conditions, you **love unconditionally**; whether those conditions be of physical attraction, social standing, goofiness, brain size, expressiveness, or whether that person threatens you or not, whatever they do or don't do, it doesn't matter; they are all the same illusion to Love. To love unconditionally means *to seek nothing* of comfort through that person to combat your own inner lack of comfort. As well, when you experience unconditional Love, you wouldn't sense another person's manners to be a testimony of your own worth, just of their own illusions, at most. And like most, you operate out of a mixed bag of identities that contributes to that through your days, don't you? In later cycles, nothing will stop these recognitions.

Today, you are trying to **leave appearances** and approach reality. So much of your unexamined life is bowing to how things appear externally. And you might even believe that it is the only natural thing in the world. Yet the only truly natural thing is sinking down and in, to self, to I Am in you. Simply concentrate on the unfailing companionship that surrounds you, from within. Unfailing companionship. Seriously. You can be your own best friend, rather than your own enemy. You can be the one showering yourself with the attention, interest, affection, and attraction you live searching the world externally for.

Today, spend time to consider all the ways you use appearances to **look outward to achieve** some state from others when that aspect is already quite within you. Talk to me when you notice these things and tell me you want deeply to hear my voice as your unfailing companion. I will listen. In that listening go down and in, and the answer will come from me to you.

Day Twenty
Trust

True relating exists truly with anyone in any way with no sense of loss. Due to your past agreements, some friends and family were born to demonstrate this to you, and you for them. Let this speak to you today. Reaffirm God's strength in you to reorient your goals in all relationships. Trust in your being.

The picture you paint can be painted within your heart.
Trust in yourself. Joy abounds whether you paint
mountains or let the warm void remain

Anytime someone feels inadequate, they've first **trusted in the possibility** of it. Due to a sense of deep concern, they've judged themselves as capable of being weak in their center and project the cause of it to the outside world, whether that cause appears now or in the past. It can be held in place by an arrogance of mind which leads into deeper ways to appease the world with gentleness and availability when others initiate. Only those with a sense of *surety* in their own weakness would latch onto this particular pseudo-solution. Any pseudo-solution is no worse or better than any other, but it is good to see another way you may give up your own awareness of God's strength in you.

Throughout life, you're given opportunities for growth, and baby faith can bloom into a much fuller acknowledgement in a single lifetime, depending on your soul evolution and any agreements you've made to manifest your full soul age in this life. The best you can ever do is to **take time to notice** this is your doing and then make peace with your pseudo-solution. After all, it was your choice to take this on. When you do this, you affirm that I Am is the strength in which you trust.

The state of your relationships seems tethered to the present or historical compatibility of those involved, whether communication is based on a gentle exchange or a brisk one. Yet, true Love as true relationship, like true strength, is not **dependent on compatibility**, for dependence is based on ego compatibility. True relating exists truly with *anyone* in *any way* with *no* sense of loss. Due to your past agreements, some friends and family were born to demonstrate this to you, and you for them. Let this speak to you today. Reaffirm God's strength in you to reorient your goals in *all* relationships.

For those who are gentle, notice how you grasp for the ease to pacify your own ego fear. Perhaps you hide from those who seem more aggressive or impulsive to maintain your own ego stability. For those who are more direct, notice how you may push those who seem too gentle or kind hoping to gain more immediate honesty. Regardless of which direction your illusion, you can **choose differently** today. Lay your arrogance down and say:

> *"I made a mistake which is not condemnable, and I can choose again once I see the true purpose of my relationships more clearly."*

You may want to say, *"I was wrong. I am sorry. I will never do it again."* But these can be changed to more honest, truthful statements by saying within:

> *"I was mistaken, I forgive myself, I see no purpose in repeating this error."*

The strength of I Am shows you this because the voice of I Am speaks to you of this.

You've known this a while, but ego-learning has come in phases for quite a long time. Let it still speak to you now here. Listen to life, which unfolds not to frighten you, but to give you **new opportunities**. Things will come up quickly today and show themselves plainly through more availability to I Am. See the bind or the double-bind you revel in for what it is: a delaying maneuver without true pleasure. Perhaps it relies on a semi-false reluctance leading to enveloping submission and finally to intense ego acceptance with resentment. Or maybe a rush to be dominant and control a situation to reduce uncertainty. It comes in a variety of forms, which we will approach in the final week. For today, acknowledge that the easy food of the ego, that sweetness, is replacing something of far greater sustenance.

Be gentle inside you and more naturally strong and spontaneous outside yourself with others. And **peace will arise** in you if you trust it. It's as simple as that. Yes, there are no streamers or balloons in this type of experience, but does this concern you? Simple, graceful glory is the only true glory. Trust in it. The ground which feels very wide is the stability of your spirit to sustain itself through the presence of I Am. This is the only sustenance you'll ever need, and one day you'll see this. For now, you may still chase the pleasures of childhood in a manner to get more peace. Pause for a moment and ask yourself, what are they for? Trust that you know the answer.

You would benefit more often from the **simplest recognition** as has occurred for you before. Recall how everything drops away. Recall the gentle sounds you did pick up. Each sound bathed you in your environment, but none distracted you. That is *trusting in your center* as the strength of God. That is peace. Today, seek within for that quiet place of self-aware Love. Look not to a deeper need or to an idol to fulfill. There is none that truly can. We assure you of this in love, not fear.

The picture you paint can be painted within your heart *on this very canvas.* You have the paints within you; trust in yourself. You may choose not to paint in the morning during your practice, yet you always have another opportunity. You always have the ability. Your doubt that **the mountains didn't paint themselves** is a doubt many of the passive sons of God have. Christ has no body now but yours. Recall this hymn? It speaks *only* of self-actualization.

In such a way, *you* are the light of Christ here. And paint as you will in the glory of creation. Joy abounds whether you paint mountains or let the warm void remain. Both are valid expressions on this plane. In the next plane you'll have such a choice, and it will be even clearer. I Am informs all choices. He animates and embodies you, even in your simplest and gentlest of activities. Rejoice then that **time**, being what it is, **is not the measure of truth** you once thought. Accomplishment is a poor yardstick for Christ's embodiment, though it may be valid for your ego.

You do not exist in time or space. Time and space arise *in* you. Sense the true yardstick: eternal being. Let go of your evaluation of things based on limits, to its own inner freedom and its own inner strength. **Trust in your being**. This is the trust in which you call to yourself today. From here, in I Am, all strength is afforded you. You sense it. No fearful questions anymore. No doubts. You are. As God Is.

Day Twenty-One
A New Beginning

Attune yourself to the highest frequency you can envision. No, you cannot learn to be the blue sky, but you can learn to be aware that this is what you are, and you can practice this awareness. You can learn how to overcome clouds through Love. Yet, you cannot learn Love, for it is what you are. This is a beginning. This is how new life begins.

Although dedicated time to reflect and meditate on the nature of the self is advised, true meditation is not a separate activity in life; it is a new way of seeing life.

For today, rest once again, and reflect on your journey before going onward. We will provide some simple context today, which we would ask you to use in your own meditation. The three-week cycle is complete, much has been covered, and so the following week will be more specific to the variety of distortions of Love your obstacles make. Obstacles distort the one energy of the higher self, producing the voice of the lower self in your experience and your faults, or darker attributes. Working with that distortion and untangling the knotted and dense material by acknowledging it concisely and sending love and acceptance to it converts that energy and transmutes the attributes into their unitive, constructive counterparts. It reunites the parts within you once hidden or separated out, and your ability to hear my voice, your higher self, increases. By making progress in your inner shadow work, the healing of the separation you perceive in the outer world automatically occurs.

You used to have the question, *"When do I meditate?"* And do you recall our answer then? Yes, always. Although dedicated time to reflect and meditate on the nature of the self is advised, **true meditation is not a separate activity** in life; it is a new way of seeing life. In fact, along with prayer, it is life itself. It may take decades to feel the presence of I Am somewhat consistently. Or it may be quick. Our advice, perform regular meditation in the morning and in the evening each day. In the morning, welcome the day as an expression of your own lifeforce. In the evening, reflect on your day to constructively acknowledge your role in all things. All meaning is attributed by you. No thought is neutral. Your thoughts provide to all things all the meaning they have for you.

During the day, **attune yourself** to the highest frequency you can envision. No, you cannot *learn* to be the blue sky, but you *can* learn to be aware that this is what you are, and you can practice this awareness. You can learn how to overcome clouds through Love. Yet, you cannot learn Love, for it is what you are. You are heaven. You are the blue sky. That is why I Am in you takes the final step, for the ego cannot take such a step. In fact, it is a non-step. And any attempt of the ego to walk through that door *makes* the door apparently walked through just another illusion, perhaps this time an illusion seemingly aligned to an image of holiness or the idea of goodness or love. The ego is that which gets you to the door and knocks. But the ego *cannot cross* through such a door.

The ego activity, in all the apparent forms it takes, will only **let go willingly** and cease its activity when it is loved and accepted. Then it no longer needs to prepare, hoard, accomplish, help, ask, catalogue, fight, or teach. One simply rests in being without an ego state overlaid on top. Or even with an overlay, the self simply rests in the activity informed by essence. It sees through the overlay pretending to be truth. The overlay is merely interpretation. The overlay is seen not to threaten self. It is only an unessential activity of self. And when the separate self is laid down, you do not take that step, for there is no you apart from I Am.

And in that moment, there *is* no step. In fact, within every deliberate step you choose lies a step seemingly away from it. Seemingly, for in mistaking the overlay for truth, *you* step away from Love. **Love is incapable of asking for anything** without losing awareness of its knowledge of itself. God asks not for a concession. And what passes for Love to the ego is more a trade-off or a hidden desire than Love itself. Consider the love of a mother for her child.

Not everything here will appeal to you equally. Some items may be easily dismissed for quite some time but will surely not remain this way. This is not surprising, as you are each still actively learning what you wish to teach. And you only teach yourself what you wish to learn yourself. Our primary advice is to **use your reactions** to the ideas within these transmissions honestly, whatever they are, with no pretense. How? Simply by noticing what arises within you. Let your thoughts, perceptions, and emotions and body sensations actively teach you who you believe yourself to be. This is the deeper lesson here, and one you were meant to learn. Whatever seems affected, notice and use it in your daily practice. Don't force the change of anything you think is advocated by, or feel would be against, the guidance within these pages. No whys are needed. Not really. Just noticing is enough.

This is a beginning. This is how new life begins.

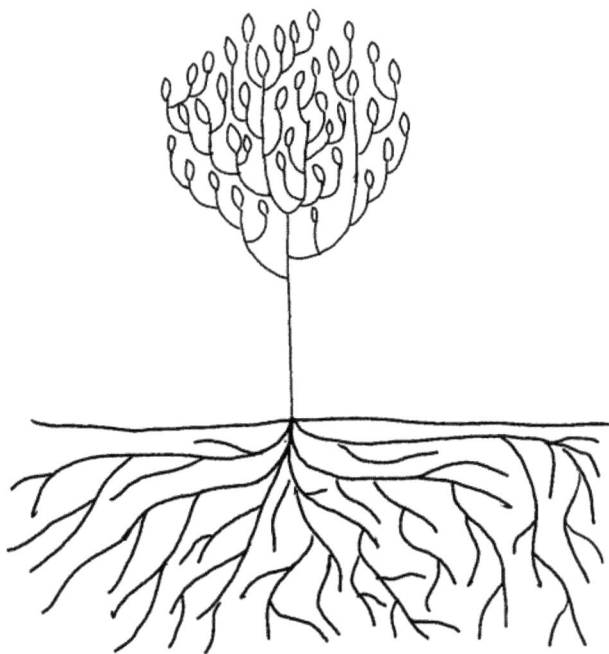

WEEK 4:
The Seven
Obstacles

Day Twenty-Two
Losing Your Center

At the center is your fear of change, or unpredictability. This takes you from your natural center where you can take in new information, and sends you fractured to the periphery where the world seems to await to strike again.

In this fear, disasters are what you collect.

Are you afraid? There is nothing to fear. How can we be so certain? We've seen this life and many others like it and lived it with you many times throughout this cycle. **Perspective changes** when one's sight is clearer. But one thing gets less clear here in the astral: amplified fear. Fear as an impetus to learning is filled with the world of matter. Thus, when fear is present you see illusions as real. We cannot, but we can relate and guide you to truth. Fear is less amplified in the next plane, the astral.

Now, we don't ask you to bake a cake in a war zone. When you see truly, you see no war. And thus, your cake is easily baked and there's ample time to share it with your bitter enemy. Today, if you lay down your fears as often as possible you will **sense the senselessness** of life lift and new purpose again resonate. Fatigue does seem real to you, doesn't it?

You've also been up and down this path of fearlessness in practice, but have **not stayed on this path** for very long, have you? The why or where you fall away from truth matters not to truth. Reaffirm the truth; I Am is a lamp unto your feet if you so look.

The seven ways to experience your fear come down from the seven energies of the divine, through the triune nature, two poles each, and a center. At the center is your **fear of change**, or unpredictability. This takes you from your natural center where you can take in new information, and sends you fractured to the periphery where the world seems to await to strike again. In this fear, disasters are what you collect.

Your own manner of relating to this obstacle is a situational **unpreparedness**, which inspires you to prepare for what disaster is looming next. It can make you frantic and fractured, fearful and struggling to comprehend new information as it arises. You become negatively inspired by fear to over-prepare in this replacing of your center. In doing so you lose your own true center and your peace.

The truth is that *there is nothing to fear*. Repeat this as often as you can throughout the day. It will always remove this splintering of your perception and the fear of perceived loss associated with it. Embracing this truth, you will flow more willingly **within your center** through each change in life, each situation. Unlike the stubborn rock at the bottom of the lake you will now lift in joy and float along with the lifeforce.

Make no mistake about it, this is a complete change of perspective when you **attune to truth** so swiftly by using these words, so expect your lower self to again fear this change as you may think it is unpredictable as well. Yet we assure you, this change is as sure as God.

For today, meditate on the **surety in God**. There is nothing to fear. Close your eyes. Fear not. Sink down into the sweet serenity of truth. There is nothing to fear.

Day Twenty-Three
Believing in Unworthiness

By removing your own worth, you open yourself up to ridicule, which you collect, not only from others, but from yourself, for all fear is internal. Your gratifying fantasies of unworthiness and worthlessness are poor substitutes for joy and the satisfaction of the good. You are worthy of the good!

Self-ridicule based on unworthiness will stop
any activity towards growth and push you
to submit to an untruth.

There is nothing to fear. What prevents you from applying this idea often throughout your day? On the action axis, two such chief fears pull you away from your true center and beg for your attention.

Underlying the first of the two, being more focused on the inner world is the idea that you are **not worth the effort**, or at least not without suffering and falling victim to your trials. This is the fear of worthlessness which informs a victim mindset. Are you really worth the effort here? Isn't a more careless approach to your day appropriate, as you're not worth the care of proper guidance?

Search yourself. You know this is not true. Yet, in your day of distracted action, it is easy to fall into a world where it seems to undermine each effort. By removing your own worth, you open yourself up to **ridicule**, which you collect, not only from others, but from yourself, for all fear is internal. Self-ridicule based on unworthiness will stop any activity towards growth and push you to submit to an untruth.

You are worthy of this work.

You do not need to search for false suffering, false submission, informed by a fearful martyr's mindset. Martyrdom in this way may inform your duties and obligations, saying, *"Oh, no one else would do this, so I must..."* or it may thwart them, saying, *"How could I be worthy of this work/effort? It's all meaningless anyway."* Under these types of expressions lie the **badge of suffering** and self-ridicule as a false treasure of life.

The purpose of this obstacle is to make your day lack any **positive expectation**. You know this is self-imposed, and can change in an instant, by seeing your false selflessness as mortification. Your gratifying fantasies of unworthiness and worthlessness are poor substitutes for joy and the satisfaction of the good. You are worthy of the good! You *are* the resurrection and the life in a *very real sense*. Repeat this earnestly and you will feel the sea-change to your mindset.

Act in a positive self-full manner today with a light heart. **Compliment your positive qualities** and constructive approach in God, and remind yourself that there is nothing to fear.

You are worthy.

Day Twenty-Four
The Belief in Missing Out

You cannot miss out on life, for life exists wherever you are. The mountain is always there for you to climb, whatever mountain you are experiencing today. The experiences you are having are valuable, even if not the most glorified or desirable to your ego.

In this fear, one is focused on the outer world around the idea of collecting disappointments.

On the action axis, the second of the chief fears is focused onto the outer world and the idea of **collecting disappointments**. When your heart is in fear of missing out, one can become so impulsive to do something, *anything*, simply to fill the time that is present. To call this obstacle impatience is to potentially confuse you, because the stereotypical behavior of rushing can be caused by any of the seven different fearful motivations.

This fear is active when the inner urgency is centered around not having the right, or enough, **experiences**. You recall as a child feeling such a way? You may have had hopes to do things, yet you were subject to your parents' constraints. These disappointments manifested as a feeling of being neglected in time, and you may have sulked in response. You may have projected the neglect onto time itself as an adult and feel this general sense that you're the hero standing up for the value of time itself! The days may be long gone where you drop your backpack at the front door afterschool and run to eat your favorite snack with muddy shoes still on. Yet, missed opportunity costs may still weigh heavy on your soul.

Even if this is not your chief fear, this obstacle may gain strength from working with any other fear, or your other obstacle on the action level, martyrdom. As those with impatience as their chief fear grow into adults, this fearful desire of missing out of experience is its own monster, which informs their greatest fearful responses. When this is so, the urgency of not acting leads to an inner intolerance, which can inform a knee-jerk desire for surprisingly **audacious behavior**. A grasping for opportunity or activity may be seen, affecting most anyone around you.

There truly is nothing to fear. You cannot miss out on life, for **life exists** wherever *you are*. The mountain is always there for you to climb, whatever mountain you are experiencing today. The experiences you are having are valuable, even if not the most glorified or desirable to your ego. The acceptance of being here now has helped you with this obstacle and can help once again.

The frantic urge to be **somewhere other than with yourself** can be confronted simply by sitting with and as yourself. You are both cart and driver. There is nowhere else to run. Today, take time to be, and see it does not rely on doing. You truly cannot miss out on being yourself. You are eternal now, regardless of what specific activity is happening in the moment.

Day Twenty-Five
The Fear of Loss of Control

Fearing annihilation often leads one into the very coping mechanisms which ironically are self-destructive themselves. This fear lies on the inner side of the expression axis and asks you for sacrifice at best or immolation at worst.

The fear of loss of control often increases on a day where many things are happening which seem out of your control or overwhelming. Such a fear causes one to collect malfunctions.

We've said it before, and we'll say it again. There is nothing to fear. All **fears are illusory** but seem quite real to you. We've covered three of the seven, so let's continue with a fourth today.

The fear of loss of control seems to be in your mind, and often increases on a day where many things are happening which seem out of your control or overwhelming. Such a fear causes one to collect malfunctions, and symptoms may arise as specific substance **addictions** or behavioral addictions like compulsive ordering and tidying of objects, over-cleaning surfaces, or compulsive thinking. **Compulsions** are a pseudo-solution to refocus you and help you feel in control of something, if even that something is trivial, and that control is a false sense of security.

The **senses are often a grounding point** as well, and so the lower bodily energies which respond closer to grounding may well be full of sensations which attempt to reduce the fear: overeating, drinking, even wishing to be consumed in compulsive exercise or sex. All this attempts to ground you to prevent being consumed in a world of seeming chaos. We assure you; it is not chaos. I Am goes with you.

Fearing annihilation often leads one into the very **coping mechanisms** which ironically are **self-destructive** themselves. This fear lies on the inner side of the expression axis and asks you for sacrifice at best or immolation at worst. There is no surprise that this fear can easily work hand in hand with martyrdom as they share similar language markers. Where martyrdom works at action level, self-destruction starves (and even substitutes for) your ability to express from the inside. Therefore, a behavior which will help remove the fear is healthy expression on any level in any form. To help understand this, we urge you to recall that fears feed behavior at motive level.

Do not get wrapped up in the ego-activity of **analyzing others**. Stay vigilant of this behavior and remind yourself often that the behaviors of others which appear fearful to you may be informed by anything, including any of the seven fears; there is no real way to tell externally. Yet a compulsive need to analyze others may be a function to compensate for the call to self-destruction within *you*.

Go within today and sit in your fear of what the loss of control within your perceived chaos may bring. **Confess your fears** to your higher self, even if they are illusory at their core, and remind yourself that there is truly nothing to fear.

You will get through today just fine, even if it is in a way that only **God knows**. That is the truth always. Each of you just pretend to know and plan accordingly. Getting out in front of things may serve an ego purpose in a variety of ways. Remember, everything can be done only by the attributes I Am gave you to communicate and act. Give thanks today for all these and ask Him for the next step each day.

Day Twenty-Six
The Fear of Lack

The impulse of true greed is unique and is felt as a burning lack within the solar plexus. When satiated, the heart center is fulfilled as immediate false-compensation, and it is this feeling which creates the fleeting gambler's high often sensed, as well as the hunger which follows just beyond it. It is the getting which is devalued and desired, the voracity of feeding, more than the accumulation when in this fear.

What were was once collected as losses, justifying lack,
are now able to be seen as what brings new opportunity.

Apart from your natural **inner abundance which sustains** you, the fear of lack speaks loudly to all during this age of materialism and intellect. This fear lies on the outer side of the expression axis, luring your attention fearfully to a hunger for enough, which appears never to be satiated for long by your world. Limited resources, losing employment, expensive services all become the focal point for decisions when in this fear. A lack of trust that I Am will provide and sustain you is evident as more is reached for in the outside world to accumulate and horde for a replacement for what your inner love couldn't properly express: your human need, perhaps for affection or material objects.

Although large collections and **large appetites** may be inspired by any of the seven fears, they are especially important to those with greed as their chief fear, of course, when they are possible. How polarizing such a need is to one's life often makes them not only unachievable, but always thirsted for, like water in the desert. When achievable, they may take center stage for creation of an identity, again as egotistic replacement therapy for some unexpressed inner voice; better, they believe, it is to feed the false need than stay wanting something they may never have. And who needs it anyway, once the largest collection of a specific item is achieved?

One need not be greedy in the true sense to grasp and take more than one's fair share of resources, but the impulse of true greed is unique and is felt as a burning lack within the solar plexus. When satiated, the heart center is fulfilled as immediate false-compensation, and it is this feeling which creates the fleeting gambler's high often sensed, as well as the hunger which follows just beyond it. When in this fear, it is the getting which is devalued and desired, the **voracity of feeding**, more than the accumulation. Conversely, the greater the loss, the greater the sense of lack is experienced, ratcheted up to a new high.

Demands for attention, common in children, continue well onto the adult years when in the grips of greed. Yet some introspection would show quite rightly that the conditions for overcoming this fear are provided for abundantly in one own's illusion. Time to sit within yourself is advised, where one speaks clearly, loudly, and honestly and actively listens to oneself about one's needs. Hearing the abundance of inner desires and fears surrounding you provides you with a sense of clarity, which then you can share with others.

This condition of **sharing the self** is the turning point. Who can share unless one already has? And what is shared except a form of Love, perhaps shrouded in fear? The fear dissipates more and more as you are heard, as your outer expressions are received without argument or denial.

What may be a desire for material objects pivots to a desire for the more subtle objects, and it is here the hunger can be more easily acknowledged as false. In time, faith in your own ability to hear and respond to your own needs replaces the desire for others to do so exclusively. **A healthy responsibility** for achieving the goals commensurate with the need is developed and maintained. What were was once collected as losses, justifying lack, are now able to be seen as what brings new opportunity from which new abundance can flourish once again. You are sustained by the Love of God.

Day Twenty-Seven
The Voice of Self-Deprecation

This fear equates you with weakness, limitation, and smallness and deceives you with false expressions of humility at your expense. True humility comes not from self-doubt, but from strength, and it costs absolutely nothing. Can you, with I Am within, be anything other than filled and abundant with His truth, His Love, and His courage?

The fear of inadequacy speaks to you of your inabilities and equates these limited views in the body with your being.

You are not a body. Of this you can be sure. Indeed, it is only insanity which speaks of you of such limited potential, for from what source could a lifeless body be animated? Yet a doubt of being able to hear your true voice, God's inspiration, informs this fear, which is an **illusion of limitation**. It denies your inner inspiration and replaces it with self-doubt and supplication to a false need for a power outside of you to support you.

God inspires you from *within* because I Am *is* within. His voice is so close to you, no matter what is happening, no matter where you are and what you are experiencing. Yet, this fear of inadequacy places God's voice outside of who you believe you are, and without it you fantasize about **being nothing**, and at best, being saved. This fear equates *you* with weakness, limitation, and smallness and deceives you with false expressions of humility at your expense. True humility comes not from self-doubt, but from strength, and it costs absolutely nothing. Can you, with I Am within, be anything other than filled and abundant with His truth, His Love, and His courage?

The fear of inadequacy speaks to you of **your inabilities** and equates these limited views in the body with your being. By misidentifying yourself in such a way, your very nature is denied without your seeing. Yet, while in this fear you can do all you want to deny I Am within, you cannot change your reality. You can deny your willpower, your ability to see clearly, your nature as pure Love for as long as squandering your being holds purpose. Yet in your fear, can you not decide to listen to me?

Hear my voice, and let it speak to you. It is **your true voice**. It is within. You can access it anytime. You can listen within and be inspired once again, to live without self-doubt, empowering you to share your being with all who as well mistake their own self. I Am speaks Love to you within. This Love ministers to all who cannot yet hear it through you or through those who do as well.

Listen and be empowered, hearing God's voice within you throughout the day. You are Love incarnate, which **recognizes its own nature** before being able to truly share it with anyone. Do not try to love or help another if you leave yourself bereft of your own being. Inspire others by first being abundantly inspired and full of your nature: God's Love.

Day Twenty-Eight
Vulnerability to Judgment

In arrogance you've placed your separate self in an unwarranted position of special authority which relies on others appreciating or at the very least agreeing with you. What if they don't? What then? You're convinced your world will fall apart as you will undoubtedly fall from your position when challenged.

This fear arises over vulnerability to judgment and collects embarrassments and humiliation. It doesn't need to rely on the eyes of others noticing you, but often does get worse in those situations.

The outward facing replacement for true inspiration relies on what you believe, or fear, the outside world thinks you are. Born from a habit of believing in your judgments of everyone and everything results in your fearing your own vulnerability to the judgments of others. Unlike self-deprecation, in arrogance you've placed your separate self in an unwarranted position of **special authority** which relies on others appreciating or at the very least agreeing with you. What if they don't? What then? You're convinced your world will fall apart as you will undoubtedly fall from your position when challenged.

One need not be outwardly boastful about one's own knowledge to be arrogant in the truest sense, although you may very well be. In many cases, outwardly boastful behavior may be motivated by any of the seven fears, including arrogance. On the other hand, a desire for perfectly orchestrated gentle cooperation through a **hypersensitivity** to your environment may be underpinned by a manicured fear of conflict arising from arrogance, and include behaviors of social isolation, hiding of your true self, or even pretending to be someone else. In this form you replace the world with your fearful projection of it and begin to expect the worst.

Whatever the form of arrogance, it arises over vulnerability to judgment, and **collects embarrassments** and humiliation. It doesn't need to rely on the eyes of others noticing you, but often does get worse in those situations, perhaps when meeting new people or the arena of public speaking. You may subconsciously think, *"I know I am no fool, but what if I make a fool of myself?"* Your idea of what others might be thinking about you may be paralyzing. For sure, you think, you cannot survive it.

This fear inspires you work incessantly to be **seen as** inhumanly perfect, or at the very least, better in comparison to peers. It's only good enough when you cannot be singled out as less. It's ideal when you receive praise for your contribution. When this fear is active, the joy of accomplishment is replaced by receipt of the right feedback or the right comments. And when highly fearful, your hypersensitivity makes almost everything others say appear as a criticism.

In the end, **appearances**, or how one is seen or thought of, dictate the action of the arrogant, whether crassly boastful or quietly hidden. Replacing the importance of the regard of others with honest self-regard in I Am, one can operate from an undefended center, no longer fearing vulnerability. Doing so requires faith that the act of exposure can be survived. Consistent exposure therapy is beneficial.

Success here means that masks are relinquished voluntarily as they serve no further constructive purpose. One begins to see that they cripple, not protect. By being inspired by I Am within you, by allowing Him to speak to you throughout your day, you can be truly available to loved ones and open with them without fear. You can **stand as who you are**, and not only as you appear to be.

APPENDIX A:
References

B̲elow, are some selections from the major works and bodies of knowledge which have positively impacted my own practice and thus inspired me in the writing of this work. They are grouped by author/channel and each group sorted by date. Wherever possible, dates reported for the creation or original transmission of the work took precedence over a specific publication date.

Rudolf Steiner	1894	Intuitive Thinking as a Spiritual Path
Ramana Maharshi	1902-1950	The Spiritual Teaching of Ramana Maharshi
Joseph Brenner	1914	The Impersonal Life
Ernest Holmes	1926-1938	The Science of Mind: The Complete Edition
Alan Watts	1951	The Wisdom of Insecurity
	1966	The Book: On the Taboo Against Knowing Who You Are
Jiddu Krishnamurti	1953	Education and the Significance of Life
	1969	Freedom from the Known
Eva Pierrakos	1957-1979	The Pathwork Guide Lectures
Helen Schucman, & Bill Thetford	1965-1972	A Course in Miracles
Shunryū Suzuki	1970	Zen Mind, Beginner's Mind
	2002	Not Always So
Sarah Chambers	1973-1985	Michael Speaks: The Legacy of Sarah Chambers
Carla L. Rueckert, Elkins, & McCarty	1981-1984	The Ra Contact: Teaching the Law of One
	2009	Living the Law of One – 101: The Choice
Jean Klein	1989-1995	The Book of Listening
Varda Hasselmann	1993	Archetypes of the Soul
	2009	The 7 Archetypes of Fear
Shepherd Hoodwin	1995	Journey of Your Soul
	1995	Loving from Your Soul
	2014	Opening to Healing
	2015	Growing through Joy
Neale Donald Walsch	1995-1998	Conversations with God, Books 1-3
Tenzin W. Rinpoche	1998	The Tibetan Yogas of Dream and Sleep
Paul Selig	2009-2010	I Am the Word
Rupert Spira	2016	Presence, Volume 1: The Art of Peace and Happiness
	2016	Presence, Volume 2: The Intimacy of All Experience
	2016	Transparent Body, Luminous World
	2017	Being Aware of Being Aware

Useful Resources:

Carl Jung	1915-1930	The Red Book: Liber Novus
Fritjof Capra	1975	The Tao of Physics
Chelsea Quinn Yarbro	1979	Messages from Michael
	1986	More Messages from Michael
Robert Baker Aitken	1982	Taking the Path of Zen
Barbara Ann Brennan	1988	Hands of Light
José Stevens	1988	The Michael Handbook
	1994	Transforming Your Dragons
John Bradshaw	1990	Homecoming: Reclaiming... Your Inner Child
Lucia Capacchione	1991	Recovery of Your Inner Child
Susan Thesenga	1993	The Undefended Self: Living the Pathwork
James Hollis	1994	Under Saturn's Shadow
Sanaya Roman	1987	Opening to Channel
James H. Austin	1998	Zen and the Brain
Jordan Peterson	1999	Maps of Meaning
Georgia Coleridge	2018	The Chakra Project
Hatch, Koprowski	2018	A CE-5 Handbook
Moira & Bert Shaw	2019	50/50 Talks: Keys to the Pathwork Guide Lectures

Works of Antiquity:

c.600 BCE	The Book of Job
c.500 BCE	Tao Te Ching
c.30-110	The Gospel of Thomas
c.90-100	The Gospel of John
c.500	The Awakening of Faith in the Absolute

Afterword

The world you see is within you, and the world you engage with outside of your body is not separate from you. You are one. We've said this before and will say it again. The activity of conflict you perceive outside of you, in an external world, while outside the person, is not outside of you in the truest sense. The effect of your awakening is real and does impact the world, we assure you. In the light of your own concern over external conflict we offer the following guidance.

First, the person who believes he is lost in a world of war can awaken from his dream and let go of his fear and projection. Shine love onto it and it dissipates, both in image and in effect. Second, each day, act according to the love you shine. Your own activity invites more to see and take part in your own recognition. Remind yourself, this is who they are as well—one with all. Be vigilant of your belief in separation. War comes not from a singular personality, nor from an evil empire unseen. It is in *your heart* and only based in fear. Fear is an activity of belief in limits being what you are, and thus what you believe you are subject to. There is *no* other root cause.

On the person level, heal yourself and pray for all others in your family, all in your community, and all your world who are lost in conflict, physical or otherwise. There is no difference to us. On the family and community level, share and shine your love in the grandest manner you can, and do this remembering the Son of God as He Is, not as he believes himself to be presently. In war, people lose themselves easily. And so, never fight against war or fight *for anything*. There is *nothing* real to fight *for*. Everything real is lost sight of by fight. And for those who are fighting internally already and hold themselves on the edge of fear, we tell you, you are not alone. God is here, as He is everywhere in all, as All, and aligned to call as many to awaken as will receive His call. Answer it yourself *fully*. This is what you are called to be.

We understand, for you there are many ego activities, based in limits, which are rooted in your constructive desire to do good. It is with clarity that often only we can look on those activities and see their own internal weakness towards setting up another regime of separation, ruled by another separate identity or organization you believe is "right" compared to another. This thinking is again rooted in ego against ego. Conciliatory measures are *not* those which tighten and bear down based on one's identity.

As far as we can advise, no advertisement of defense is any less destructive to inner peace than an open act of war is, *once you see who you truly are*. Have you seen? Or do you not want to see?

To forcefully disarm another in love, is a contradiction so long as someone can be blamed for prohibiting the will of another. For this reason, Love remains itself only unseen in aggression or fully seen in acts of unification and conciliation. The simplest acts of *seeing another*, no matter how egregious their actions appear, and ministering effectively to their own illusion through a *grand outpouring of clear love based on our unity* can call many who are ready to heal themselves. This is the only true miracle, when chosen. And it costs nothing in reality—you are asked to lay down only the fantasy of division you believed in.

Don't give into the temptation to think you've effectively done this in your own efforts trying to fight for a cause. Rather, stand for truth unashamed, in the One Light of peace knowing you truly cannot lose your true self. Any growth is planted in the soil of Love, nurtured with the unified sunlight of the Holy Spirit, and watered with the lifeforce.

Your world, in your present density, has been given a chance to find a new way. Through this book, we implicitly ask you to reconsider how you contribute to war in your own lives today, and for each who hear the call to take action by seeing anew. The practice of any meditation is a direct practice of laying down your *own weapons* in the strength of love, not out of ego weakness, and it is *more powerful than you know*. Laying them down in strength liberates, laying them down in weakness self-imprisons. You only fool yourself in claiming you do not see the difference. The only difference is *who you believe yourself to truly be*.

Fear not. For there you lose sight of Love as your very being. We send all in your density our love and assure you, you are never alone in the AllOne.

(channeled February 25, 2022)

www.ingramcontent.com/pod-product-compliance
Lightning Source LLC
Chambersburg PA
CBHW071759090426
42737CB00012B/1875